Invisible Latin America

LATIN AMERICA

Invisible Latin America

by Samuel Shapiro

BEACON PRESS   **BOSTON**

Published simultaneously in Canada by
S. J. Reginald Saunders and Co., Ltd., Toronto

Printed in the United States of America

The author gratefully acknowledges permission to re-
print here portions of his articles which first appeared
in the following journals: *The Centennial Review of
Arts and Sciences, Columbia University Forum, Commentary* and the American Jewish Committee, *Dissent,
The Nation, The New Republic,* and *Studies on the
Left.*

For Gloria

Contents

Contents

Preface

This book is a product of a Fulbright Professorship to teach American Civilization and Literature at the University of Tucumán, Argentina, in 1959. At that time, like most American historians, I knew very little about the geography and history of the vast area that lies below the Rio Grande. The air journey to the province of Tucumán (with stopovers) was a useful introduction to the area, although too quick and comfortable to be as informative as similar journeys were in previous centuries. On the outskirts of Lima I saw for the first time the poverty in which so many Latin Americans live, far worse than anything of the kind in the United States. It came as a surprise to me that São Paulo is as big and modern as Los Angeles and growing even faster, and that six of Argentina's twenty million people live in Greater Buenos Aires.

Tucumán itself, located in Argentina's far north, in the sugar country, afforded further insight into the current condition of Latin America. The technological revolutions in industry and agriculture that are reshaping the rest of the continent and the world are just beginning to reach this region. All the sugar mills (*ingenios*) in the province, for example, are from thirty to sixty years old—contemporary with the steel plants that Andrew Carnegie built, or with the factories in which Henry Ford turned out the Model T. In visiting them I saw the reality of early industrial society, with all its crudeness, wastefulness, and danger; for me it was a phase of history taken out of the books and made alive.

The sugar mills reminded me of the United States early in this century; the cane fields took me even further back, to the ante-bellum South. In Tucumán, as in Louisiana before the Civil War, cane is planted, cultivated, and entirely hand-harvested with *machetes*. To take it from the fields to the *ingenios* the farmers in some places still use the *carreta*, the high-wheeled, ox-drawn wooden cart for which Tucumán was already well-known in the seventeenth century. To watch this painfully slow and inefficient process was to look once again at living history, and to understand how urgent it is for Latin America to modernize her agriculture and to make a more humane use of her human resources. Nobody profits from unskilled hand labor. Production per acre and per man-hour is very small, wages are low, profits are low and in some years nonexistent, and yet Argentines pay double the world market price for their sugar. After seeing how the sugar workers lived I understood why they were General Perón's enthusiastic supporters during his dictatorship, and why they remained loyal to him after his fall.

My observations were by no means confined to Tucumán. Latin American universities are generous with time off for rest, research, or the second job which is almost universal for their faculty members. I used my leisure for travelling in the North, to regions few Argentines and almost no Americans ever visit. On one trip I went up to Salta, perhaps the most charming city in all Argentina, with its many buildings dating from the colonial era. Salta, on the high road to the silver mines at Potosí, was once many times larger than the struggling seaport village of Buenos Aires. On this same journey I stopped for a week at a sugar plantation near the Bolivian border, and saw Churupí and Mataco Indian laborers fresh from the Chaco forests, their faces painted blue, and just beginning to wear trousers, shirts, and shoes. To see them on the day they were paid and sent back to their villages, delightedly buying hand mirrors, cheap knives, and bright bits of cloth, was to be taken back to the days of Columbus and Cortés. The only difference was that some of the Indians were buying radios and bicycles—although there are no roads or electricity in their homes along the Pilcomayo.

My homeward journey brought me sharply back to the twentieth century. I visited the booming oil fields at Campo

Duran, where American, Argentine, Japanese, and Italian companies were all at work with the most modern drilling and pipeline laying equipment, and I toured the new Kaiser plant in Córdoba, where the first Argentine automobiles were being manufactured. With the airplane's aid it was possible to span centuries in a matter of days. One week I stopped over in Brasília, an achingly new vision of the planned city of the future; the next I travelled through villages in the Peruvian Andes near Cuzco not much changed from the days of the Inca Empire.

After returning to the United States, I wanted to write about the social and economic changes I had seen taking place in South America. I continued to read about the area, and began to write for the London *Economist*, and later for the *New Republic*, *The Nation*, *The Reporter*, *Commentary*, *Dissent*, *Columbia University Forum*, and other magazines. I made three trips to Cuba, between 1960 and 1962, and wrote about the revolutionary changes taking place on that island. From these articles, and with the gentle encouragement of the Beacon Press, the present book was written.

As a newcomer to Latin American studies I have profited greatly from books, lectures, and conversations with specialists in the field. With due acknowledgement I have borrowed ideas and interpretations from such experts as Robert J. Alexander, of Rutgers University; Charles W. Arnade, of the University of South Florida; Donald Dozier, of Stanford University; Russell H. Fitzgibbon, whose Center of Latin American Studies at U.C.L.A. publishes the indispensable *Statistical Abstract of Latin America;* Hubert Herring, whose *History of Latin America* (1961) is equally useful for reading or reference; Ronald Hilton, Director of the Institute of Hispanic American and Luso-Brazilian Studies at Stanford and editor of the monthly *Hispanic American Report;* John J. Johnson, of Stanford; Manuel Lizondo Borda, of the University of Tucumán; Herbert L. Matthews, of the *New York Times;* Thomas G. Matthews, of the University of Puerto Rico; C. Wright Mills, whose untimely death cut short a growing interest in Latin American affairs; Peter R. Nehemkis, Jr., of the Whirlpool Corporation; Frederick B. Pike, of the

University of Notre Dame; Robert F. Smith, of the University of Rhode Island; Robert Taber; Luis Gomez Wanguemert, editor of *El Mundo*, Havana, and many other college teachers, government officials, editors, and Latin Americans from every walk of life. The best part of this book is based on their suggestions and emendations; the mistakes and misinterpretations, of course, are my own.

SAMUEL SHAPIRO

University of Notre Dame
South Bend, Indiana
September, 1963

CHAPTER 1

Invisible Latin America

There are two [Latin] Americas: the visible and the invisible. The visible [Latin] America . . . of presidents and embassies, expresses itself through official organs, through a controlled press. This America takes its seat at the conference table of the Pan-American Union and has many votes in the United Nations. And there is the mute, repressed America, which is a vast reservoir of revolution. . . . Nobody knows exactly what these 150,000,000 silent men and women think, feel, dream, or await in the depths of their being.

Germán Arciniegas,
The State of Latin America (1952)

Relatively few Americans ever visit the Latin American countries with which we share this hemisphere. Mexico and the Caribbean islands have a sizeable tourist industry, but there must be a dozen Americans who have travelled in France and England for every one who knows Argentina, Chile, Paraguay, or Peru. Those who do go to South America generally see only the attractive tourist folder side of life in the big cities: the modern airports, the expensive hotels, the impressive new buildings. No American city is as immaculate as Lima, where the streets are swept twice a day; no bathing place is as spectacularly beautiful as Rio's Copacabana beach, where the mountains march right down to the sea; few shopping centers are as modern or as fashionable as Florida Street in Buenos Aires.

This impression of prosperity is strengthened by the image of a pleasant, idealized Latin America promulgated until very

1

recently by journalists, advertising agencies, and Latin diplomats. The view of that region presented in American newspapers and magazines has been predominantly one of substantial material progress and occasional almost comic opera revolutions, all imposed upon a background of picturesque scenery and Hispanic charm. Much has been made of the ending of dictatorships in half a dozen countries during the past ten years and the coming to power of liberal statesmen such as José Figueres, Rómulo Betancourt, and Alberto Lleras Camargo. We see and read a great deal about the Alliance for Progress and its impressive plans for industrialization, social reform, and inter-American economic assistance. The glowing standard for this view of contemporary Latin America is the much-publicized new capital of Brasília, with its handsome modern buildings springing from the red dirt of the Goiás plateau. Except for a few "trouble spots" such as British Guiana and Fidel Castro's Cuba, inter-American relations seem amiable, and conferences of the Organization of American States are almost always reported in our press as having brought about harmonious agreement as to future economic and political cooperation in this hemisphere.

Despite their urgent requests for economic aid, Latin American governments, like most governments, are anxious to conceal from their visitors the poverty that lurks just a short distance from the wide avenues and the gleaming new buildings. With the famous exception of Vice-President Nixon's tour, good-will visits by American officials are brief and carefully arranged to avoid the disagreeable. The usual itinerary skirts South America's rural backwaters and sprawling urban slums; under the state of siege in effect in some of the countries visited, thousands of "leftists" and "agitators" were jailed until the *Yanqui* presidents were safely out of reach. Many well-to-do Latin Americans themselves are still only half aware of the bitter poverty that surrounds their pleasant lives, or else accept it as part of the natural order of things. The result has been a tendency to pass over in silence the awkward truth about the "mute, repressed America" of which Professor Arciniegas speaks.

In fact, most of the countries in Latin America have been

slipping toward catastrophe ever since the ending of the Korean War and the subsequent decline of world commodity prices. Behind the facade of spectacular new buildings is a continent sunk in hunger and misery, an area where productivity and living standards are not keeping pace with the rapid increase in population. Only a few statistics are needed to suggest the depth of the problems:

The average daily diet in Peru contains 1900 calories.

It costs the Bolivian government mining monopoly between $1.40 and $2.10 to produce a pound of tin, the country's principal export commodity; the current world price is about $1.20. The *boliviano* is currently worth less than one-hundredth of a cent.

In Argentina, Bolivia, and Paraguay, the cost of living rose between 2 and 3 per cent a month throughout 1961; in Brazil the increase was 4 to 5 per cent.

Twenty-four million Mexicans (out of a total population of thirty-five million) live in homes without electric lights.

Only half of the children between 5 and 18 are attending school; in rural areas the figure is 1 in 4. The illiteracy rate ranges from 13 per cent in Argentina to 70 per cent in Guatemala and 89 per cent in Haiti (vs. 2 per cent in the United States). Only 1 child in 20 completes a grade school education.

The wealthiest 2 per cent of the population owns 75 per cent of all arable land and 50 per cent of all personal wealth.

Thirty million urban Latin Americans live without city-controlled drinking water.

Life expectancy at birth ranges from 33 years in Haiti to 39 years in Brazil and 57 years in Argentina (vs. 67 years in the United States).

Only 3 of the 20 Latin American nations have per capita national incomes higher than $500 a year.

Latin American gold and dollar holdings fell from $3.7 billion in 1956 to $2.8 billion in 1961 and $2.3 billion in 1962, an amount "at the bare minimum necessary for financing international payments."

Latin American per capita income is only $325 a year, and has not risen at all since 1957.

These statistics represent great and growing human misery. In my travels in highland Peru it seemed to me that the Indian peasants were worse off than their ancestors had been under the intelligent despotism of the Inca. Squeezing their subsistence from small patches of sharply sloping land, barefoot, hungry, living in unheated huts with dirt floors, these Andean farmers could entertain no rational hope for better lives. Americans who have seen the fine film *Black Orpheus* had a glimpse of the *favellas,* the wretched shanty towns that cling to the sides of Rio de Janeiro's beautiful green mountains; but, art aside, these picturesque shacks have no running water or toilets, and the people who must live in them are chronically hungry and diseased. In northern Argentina, I met migrant Indian laborers who earned less than a dollar a day, lived in filthy shacks made of sugar cane stalks, and chewed on cane stalks to still their hunger. Venezuela, with its immense oil reserves, has the highest per capita income in Latin America. But none of the oil profits have "trickled down" to the people who live in the dreadful slums on the outskirts of Caracas. Even Argentina, long an example of Latin American progress and prosperity, has suffered for years from a stationary or declining gross national product, chronic deficits despite a budget that takes 30 per cent of the national income, a skyrocketing foreign debt, and—incredibly—shortages of beef and wheat!

Latin American poverty is, of course, an old story, one that goes back to the centuries of Spanish rule. With the countries to the south of us swept, however, by the same "revolution of rising expectations" that is in evidence in all the underdeveloped areas of the world, Americans must no longer ignore or underestimate its consequences. Over the course of the next decade or two the hitherto invisible mass will find its leaders and somehow heave itself into prominence. And the example of Castro's Cuba warns us that the coming social revolution may take a totalitarian, pro-Communist line; every one of the new executives installed in Brazil, Ecuador, and British Guiana in 1961 was closer than his predecessor to Castro and Khrushchev.

It is to combat this menace that we have inaugurated the Alliance for Progress, a ten-year plan for economic aid to Latin America which President Kennedy has called "a vast effort, un-

paralleled in magnitude and nobility of purpose." The United
States has announced its willingness to join commodity stabilization programs for Latin American exports, to make loans to gov-
ernment-owned enterprises, and to provide billions of dollars in
development funds to those countries prepared to improve their
own institutions. At the Punta del Este meeting in 1961, U.S.
Treasury Secretary Douglas Dillon formally committed the
United States to help bring about a 2.5 per cent per capita increase in annual income in Latin America. It is therefore essential for us to understand the obstacles that have kept Latin
America so backward for such a long time and that may render
our assistance useless.

In the first place, and despite the golden dreams that have
beguiled investors for centuries, Latin America is not a very rich
area geographically. From an economic point of view the whole
continent is shaped wrong, with the widest expanses in the huge
and all but useless Amazon basin, and comparatively thin, tap-
ering sections in the temperate zones. Northern Mexico, the region most familiar to American tourists, is a stony desert; only
10 per cent of the country as a whole is arable. Great sections
of South America's west coast are utterly arid and quite unin-
habitable. Other stretches of the continent are taken up by the
Andes, far higher than the Rockies and immensely difficult to
penetrate. Almost all of South America's great cities lie on the
rim of the continent and depend for their existence on the export
of a handful of minerals and agricultural products; the area has
few counterparts to such inland manufacturing centers as Chicago, Detroit, St. Louis or Cleveland. Despite ambitious plans
in Brazil, Bolivia, and Peru, the back country remains empty;
Brasília represents, in fact, an almost desperate effort to populate
the interior and that effort has not yet shown any sign of success.
The continent has varied mineral resources, but for the most part
lacks usable reserves of coal and iron; where these do exist, they
are generally located too far apart to permit the establishment of
heavy industry.

Added to these physical handicaps are political ones. The
United States very early in its history developed a stable, work-

able government, with a reliable currency, freedom of internal trade, property guarantees, and freedom of enterprise. But Latin America, after the revolutions of 1810–1824, speedily fell apart into more than a dozen unstable, independent entities, at war within themselves and with each other. The history of almost every country below the Rio Grande is a dismal record of *caudillos*, revolutions, and wars; under these unsettling circumstances, the rapid growth that has characterized the United States economy could not take place.

Latin American development has also been handicapped by the area's division into national states too small to function effectively as economic units. Each nation strives, foolishly, for self-sufficiency, and the result is poverty for all; it is as if New York, Massachusetts, and Michigan tried to protect themselves against neighboring states by an elaborate system of tariffs, quota restrictions, and currency control. Customs regulations are complex and administered with infuriating inefficiency. I recall, for example, that it cost me an entire working day to get a small box of microfilm from the United States into Buenos Aires; while I waited I saw shipments of fruit from Brazil rotting on the docks for want of an import permit, and cargoes of American automobiles and machinery that had been rusting away for months. Customs unions in Central and South America have been proposed ever since the wars of independence against Spain, but it is only in the last few years that anything effective has been done.

One reason for this lack of cooperation among Latin Americans is the festering memory of ancient rivalries and border disputes. The Argentine-Chilean squabble over a few Atlantic islands, Bolivian and Paraguayan memories of the bitter Chaco war of the 1930's, the rivalry between Brazil and Argentina for hegemony over Paraguay, the perpetual brushfire wars, invasions, and revolutions all around the Caribbean, all create a climate of fear and suspicion that makes economic cooperation in the new Western European style impossible.

These rivalries, generally over territories of little intrinsic importance, serve as an excuse for the outrageous proliferation of armies and armaments in nations far too poor to afford either. No major Latin American country has fought a war in this century; there is no prospect of one in the foreseeable future, and armed aggression by an extra-hemispheric power is even less likely. Nevertheless, every nation except one or two maintains an expensive standing army, which takes from 25 per cent of the budget (in Peru, Chile, and Argentina) to over 50 per cent (in Paraguay). Brazil, with annual deficits of 40 billion *cruzeros*, spends 30 per cent of its budget (over 1 billion dollars) on a useless army, and deals with runaway inflation by giving its generals and admirals 100 per cent pay increases. Argentina has 10,000 officers on active duty, 20,000 more retired at full pay, and almost as many generals as the United States; even little El Salvador has *sixteen generals*. Overall, a burdensome expenditure of 2 billion dollars a year buys nothing but impressive officers' clubs, ridiculous navies, and splendid uniforms. Yet when Argentina's President Arturo Frondizi, forced to impose an austerity program on the rest of the nation, murmured for a modest reduction in military expenditures, he was imperiously told that the Argentine army could not afford to discharge a single soldier. Venezuela's Rómulo Betancourt similarly finds his plans for social reform and economic development hampered by the fact that he dare not cut his country's swollen military budget.

An even greater hindrance to economic progress is the social structure of Latin America, inherited from Spain and rather richly embroidered in some countries with racial antipathies. Between the well-to-do and the great masses of the poor there is in most countries only a very small and still largely powerless middle class. In Mexico, for example, 100,000 prosperous individuals at the top of the social pyramid received thirty-six billion *pesos* in income; at the bottom, ten million workers and peasants got only twenty-eight billion *pesos* (less than $250 apiece). It is still possible in many countries to hire a maid for $10 a month and board. In highland Peru and Bolivia, in the Amazon basin, in the hill country of Ecuador, Mexico, Haiti, Argentina, and Venezuela, millions of people live outside the money economy altogether.

The difficulty of bringing change to these regions must be experienced to be appreciated: one group of experts spent months trying to teach a village of Indians to boil their drinking water —in vain. On a sugar plantation I visited in the Argentine province of Salta, not a single Indian, out of a working force of nearly three thousand, was able to read or write; even the *caciques* signed their contracts with an "X." The law is obeyed, but not put into effect: when I asked an overseer why there were no schools on the plantation, he smiled and told me that "these *peones* can cut cane just as well without being able to read and write." In Mexico, one of the most advanced countries in the area, two people out of five are still illiterate; a few years ago President Ruiz Cortines had to admit that the revolution had brought few benefits to the "enormous masses who still suffer in ignorance, enduring poverty and unhealthful conditions."

As the example of Spain—that most un-European of nations —shows, the Hispanic attitude toward life positively militates against material progress. Even educated Latin Americans seem to lack the drive and entrepreneurial skill required to build an industrial civilization. The badly-managed and unproductive *hacienda* provides for its owner a comfortable way of life, with few worries, much leisure, and an abundance of cheap household help. He derives from it some cash income, which he is likely to invest in urban real estate—or in Wall Street or Switzerland— and he is definitely not interested in becoming a rival to some North American millionaire. When American captains of industry like Rockefeller, Carnegie, and Ford made money, they reinvested it and set about making more, a process that led to mass production, economy of scale and huge industries. For the South American, on the other hand, business has never been an end in itself, but only a way to get enough money to enjoy life. My friends in Peru were incredulous when I assured them that Nelson Rockefeller's motive in running for office was not related to his private fortune: "You mean he has all that money and really doesn't *have* to work?"

As a consequence of this psychological attitude, and the recurrent political instability that makes it impossible to plan for the long future, few businessmen in Argentina or Chile drive themselves in the manner of a nineteenth-century American captain of industry or a contemporary "Organization Man." The ideal is to accumulate a fortune, preferably in farm land or city apartments that can be handled by a manager, large enough to live on comfortably. The aim of life is the intelligent enjoyment of leisure. Some of my own Yankee graduate-school enthusiasm for hard work was speedily blunted in South America, where one learns to enjoy an easier tempo. There is indeed much to be said for the cultural values of friendship, the contemplative life, and "sweetly doing nothing." For the Latin American middle and upper classes, life has always been easy and servants cheap; it is hard to sell washing machines, vacuum cleaners, and other labor-saving devices where servants will do all the chores for a few dollars a month. But the habit of looking on work as debasing must be considered a handicap to the forming of a society that would provide some leisure for everybody and not just for the few.

Even the most energetic Latin American businessman is faced with obstacles that are likely to blunt his enthusiasm and lessen his chances of success. Argentine employers I spoke to invariably complained of the difficulty of getting skilled and willing workers. Even those they trained themselves were generally resentful of their status as wage earners, and under the control of an essentially political labor union. They worked with a vexing lack of energy and efficiency, and when they went on one of their frequent strikes, terrorism and bombings were (and are) normal weapons.

Some enthusiastic advocates of the Alliance for Progress have argued that it can achieve the same results as the Marshall Plan in Europe, that a few billion dollars worth of pump priming will bring about another "German Miracle" in Argentine and Brazil. But, among other things, the elaborate network of transportation and communication that is taken for granted in advanced industrial countries simply does not exist in South America; a bitter strike of sugar workers in the Argentine province where I was teaching some years ago was prolonged for a number of days because the governor of the province was *unable to reach the authorities in Buenos Aires by telephone.* Millions of man-hours are wasted by slow and cumbersome bank, postal, and delivery procedures; as a visiting Yankee, I soon enough learned to shrug, smile, and agree with the proverb: "Patience, and the grass will become milk." Throughout Latin America roads are bad, automobiles are ancient, and a railroad journey of any length is generally an ordeal of dirt, discomfort, and delay. Even the most modern means of transportation are disappointingly slow. On half a dozen airline flights within Argentina, for example, I was delayed anywhere from six to thirty hours, and my English-speaking Argentine friends laughingly quoted another maxim: "If you have time to spare, go by air."

Economic growth is bound to be severely undercut, of course, if honest and stable government is lacking. Experience shows that a modern industrial state can be brought into being under a system of parliamentary democracy or under the forced draft of a dictatorship. But an intricate web of economic relationships cannot be built up under governments that change every few years, waste enormous amounts in unproductive expenditures, and damage their economies by inefficiency, inflation, and graft on a gigantic scale. The postwar dictatorships in Latin America came into power when high prices for sugar, beef, oil, and coffee had filled national treasuries, and they stole and squandered staggering amounts. In Cuba alone, in seven years, Fulgencio Batista and his henchmen made away with the better part of a billion dollars, and this amount is small compared to the sums squandered or stolen by dictators who looted wealthier Argentina and Venezuela. What they did not steal, they wasted; Latin America is littered with the costly marble monuments of Odría, Perón, Pérez Jiménez, Trujillo, and the rest—Machado's $18 million capitol in Havana peering across to a $50 million University City in the Argentine Andes to which not a single student has ever been admitted. Democratic regimes are sometimes the worst. Juscelino Kubitschek's Brasília cost half a billion dollars in construction costs alone, while the *cruzero* plummeted to less than half a cent and hunger stalked the neglected northeast coast, where per capita income is less than $100 a year. Lending or giving money to governments like these is a highly inefficient way of aiding Latin America's masses—like overfeeding horses to make sure the birds get enough to eat.

Since the end of the Korean War, the inflated commodity prices that fed Latin America's white elephants have collapsed, leaving her one-crop economies deeply depressed. Copper, for example, fell from 44 cents a pound in 1955 to 25 cents in 1958; sugar dropped 50 per cent in price between 1954 and 1959. Brazilian coffee exports rose from 11 million sacks in 1954 to 17.5 million sacks in 1960, but price declines during the same period cut her income from $948 million to $750 million.

The average North American is simply not aware of the economic disaster that these statistics represented for his neighbor to the south. In a number of countries the gross national product is practically stationary, and in a few it has actually declined in recent years, while population continues to climb at a rate of 2.4 per cent a year (as compared to an average 1.6 per cent for the rest of the world). Should existing trends continue—there is no reason why they should not—the area's present population of 190 million will increase to 300 million by 1975. In a number of rural areas I have visited in Bolivia, Peru, Mexico, and Argentina, the population is already living at just about the subsistence level.

The forebodings of Malthus are reality in such places; there is no place for the younger men to go but to join the unemployed in La Paz, Lima, Mexico City, and Buenos Aires. Here they stagnate in one of the *villas miserias, villas diablos,* or *callejones* that surround most Latin American metropolises. The rapid growth of many cities is thus a sign of economic distress, and not of prosperity. Lima, for example, has doubled in population since the end of World War II not because of normal economic growth, but because it is an uneasy resting place for Indians spilling down from the mountain villages.

As this list of geographic, social, and psychological obstacles to the success of the Alliance for Progress makes clear, achieving rapid and democratically-oriented economic · growth in Latin

America will not be easy. We have called upon the area's ruling classes to give up some of their wealth and special privileges, but we have no way to compel them to do so; we can only promise—Congress willing—to aid them if they do reform. While American diplomacy can exert considerable pressure in the right direction, our government is obviously unable to bring about by fiat the changes in social structure, political institutions, and economic attitudes that are urgently required. That is a job for the Latin American ruling classes themselves, and they do not seem particularly eager to get on with it. Nor can we or our partners in the Alliance do anything about bringing rain to the western deserts, lowering the Andes, or changing the rainy tropical climate of the Amazon basin.

We must realize, then, that we are not omnipotent and that there are limits to what even the ablest diplomacy in Washington can accomplish. The Alliance for Progress can achieve even limited success only if it is a true partnership, and not a panicky series of loans and grants that will have no more permanent effect than a handout to an alcoholic beggar. The hope inspired by Washington's new and noble intentions should be qualified and realistic, and the essential factor in whatever success our policymakers can achieve is an understanding of the true state of Latin America today.

CHAPTER 2

The Stages of Latin American Growth

*Time is short. Latin America is in a revolutionary mood. It
has a great deal to change. It is far too late for a slow-paced
revolution.*

José Figueres

Most textbook descriptions of Latin America begin with a
warning: Latin America is not a cohesive, easily understood
unity. With a population roughly equal to that of the United
States and an area two and a half times larger, Latin America
presents far greater geographic, economic, social, and linguistic
variation than our own country. The region contains trackless
deserts, towering mountain ranges, tropical jungles, and three of
the world's ten largest cities. Its population is for the most part
abysmally poor by American standards, yet the Latin millionaire
is a fixture on the international scene—with no income tax to
pay. The countries range in size from Brazil, with an area larger
than the United States without Alaska, to diminutive El Salvador, the same size as Massachusetts and with half as many people. Mexico City, São Paulo, and Buenos Aires have impressive
universities and a lively intellectual life, but fifty million Latin
American adults are illiterate, and millions of them cannot speak
Spanish or Portuguese. The economic, social, and psychological
distance between a landholding aristocrat like Peru's former
President Manuel Prado and the impoverished Quechua-speak-
ing Indians who work on his plantations is simply unknown in
the United States.

13

Yet there is such a thing as a Latin American personality and social milieu; as a friend of mine described it, on his trip to Europe, "We forgot all about being Argentines, Chileans, and *Uruguayos* as soon as the boat sailed. Even the Brazilians just seemed to be speaking Spanish with a thick accent." In the United Nations, at meetings of the Organization of American States, at scholarly conferences, even in the arts, similar problems and similar ways of looking at them are evident. The developing European Economic Community demonstrates the same kind of supra-national unity that is instinctively felt from Cape Horn to the Rio Grande.

Aside from their Hispanic heritage and common history, the salient features of all twenty nations to the south of us are their poverty and the insecure state of such wealth as they do have. Despite remarkable industrial growth in a handful of favored cities since the end of World War II, Latin America as a whole remains rural, underdeveloped, and overspecialized in one or two export crops. In the following table the Latin countries are classified according to per capita national income; the parentheses show the principal exports of nations receiving more than half their export earnings from one or two products. The per capita annual income in the United States is above $2200.

Per capita national income over $700
Venezuela (Oil, 92 per cent)

Per capita national income $300–$699
Argentina
Chile (Copper and nitrates, 76 per cent)
Costa Rica (Coffee and bananas, 86 per cent)
Panama (Bananas and cacao, 72 per cent)
Uruguay (Wool and meat, 68 per cent)

Per capita national income $200–$299
Colombia (Coffee and oil, 92 per cent)
Cuba (Sugar and tobacco, 83 per cent) (1959)
Mexico

Per capita national income $100–$199

Brazil (Coffee and cacao, 64 per cent)
Dominican Republic (Sugar and cacao, 65 per cent)
Ecuador (Bananas and coffee, 75 per cent)
El Salvador (Coffee and cotton, 88 per cent)
Guatemala (Coffee and bananas, 85 per cent)
Honduras (Bananas and coffee, 70 per cent)
Nicaragua (Coffee and cotton, 73 per cent)
Paraguay
Peru

Per capita national income less than $100

Bolivia (Tin and lead, 71 per cent)
Haiti (Coffee and sisal, 80 per cent)

Depressing as they are to contemplate, these statistics still understate Latin American poverty because they do not indicate the extremely uneven distribution of national incomes and the absence of an equitable tax system. When averaged together, the income of a Chilean or Nicaraguan *hacendado* and his workers is low enough, but the owner may be getting, tax free, $50,000 or the equivalent a year and his workers must manage to exist somehow on close to nothing. The annual income of Simon I. Patiño, for example, was for some years as large as the budget of the Bolivian government; the private fortunes of the Trujillo family in the Dominican Republic and the Somoza brothers in Nicaragua are larger than the national income of their countries. In Venezuela, the oil boom has created dozens of millionaires and stranded hundreds of thousands of unemployed slum-dwellers on the outskirts of Maracaibo and Caracas. As the statistics show, Venezuela is by far the "wealthiest" nation in Latin America, with a per capita income almost equal to that of Mississippi, the poorest of American states. But two-thirds of the population is illiterate, 300,000 farmers are without land, and two per cent of the rural population owns three-quarters of the farm land. Despite dollar revenues of $100 million a month, President Betancourt has had to devalue the *bolívar* and would be bankrupt without a steady series of loans from abroad.

It is worth noting that pre-Castro Cuba occupied a place nearer the top than the bottom of the list for per capita income; the very poor seldom make revolutions. At the lowest social levels there is a fatalistic acceptance of things as they are. Here is what a Peruvian peasant told Richard W. Patch of the American University Field Service:

Our destiny depends on divine will. Because God wills it some are rich, some know how to read and write, some are masters while we are the servers . . . We are blind ignorant brutes [*chunchos*] because God has permitted it to be so. He has permitted this hacienda to exist, and that we be its servants.

The centuries-old social structure that produced and in turn rested upon this stolid and uncomplaining attitude is fast breaking up all over Latin America and the rest of the underdeveloped world. The farm laborer who looks up from his foot-plow may see a tractor in a neighboring field or a jet airplane overhead. He may be forced off the land by farm machinery or overpopulation, or he may be drawn to the city by demagogic promises or the hope of a factory job. Even if he stays where he is, he is inevitably drawn into the currents of the modern world. Political campaigns, Hollywood movies, ideological messages from Moscow, Peking, Havana, and Washington and the example of successful social revolutions in Mexico, Bolivia, and Cuba are reaching even the remotest rural backwaters. And despite their vastly different formulas for change, *fidelismo* and the Alliance for Progress both agree that change is necessary, desirable, and inevitable.

The drive for change comes from the rising middle class of professionals, technicians, and skilled workers, all of whom modern society demands and produces. Most Latin American revolutionary movements have been initiated not by the peasantry, but by dissatisfied members of the middle class: Francisco Madero,

of an enormously wealthy Mexican family of *hacendados;* Víctor
Paz Estenssoro, a Bolivian professor of economics; Juan José
Arévalo, a Guatemalan professor of philosophy; and Fidel Castro, son of a rich landholder in Oriente province and graduate
of the Law School at Havana University. It is men like these,
young, energetic, and idealistic, who lead the assault on the old
elites, the landholders, the Church, the military, the foreign investors, the ruling classes out of which they come and with
whom they might have allied themselves.

The reason some young intellectuals choose the path of revolution are many and mingled. In Fidel Castro, who married into
a family of *batistianos* and could have chosen to enjoy life under
the dictatorship, we see the typical middle class revolutionary,
in whom Messianic dreams, a thirst for personal power, and a
burning sense of social justice are inextricably mixed together.
Other threadbare young university students may look on revolution as the only way to personal advancement. In a one-crop
economy controlled by a few dozen families, politics is the only
career open to talent, and there are always more applicants than
places to fill. Some of the political conservatism and social stability of Great Britain and the United States has been owing to
the openings provided for ambitious young men in India, in the
West, or in the expanding economy; their counterparts in Nicaragua, Panama, and Argentina today may see no future open to
them except by destruction of the existing social order.

Given the area's almost overwhelming problems, made acute
by population pressure and the slump in commodity prices, we
should be able to understand why many Latin American labor
leaders, leftist politicians, young intellectuals, and even junior
army officers are coming to feel that gradual democratic reforms
are inadequate, that a *fidelista*-style social revolution (with or
without Soviet backing) is the only way. While each of the
twenty republics is distinct by reasons of local variations in geography and economic development, and by the impact of individual personalities (always important in Hispanic countries), it is
possible to classify them according to the political stage they

have reached. Readers who are familiar with the intricacies of Latin American politics will, I hope, excuse the necessary blurring of distinctions that such a listing requires.

1. *Old Style Caudillo Regimes.* The paternalistic *caudillo,* a modern counterpart of the medieval duke or count, has been a familiar fixture in Latin America since the wars of independence. He generally owns large tracts of land, has a share of many basic industries, and runs his country as if it were his personal property. He treats his people like children in need of his constant severe tutelage, and is sometimes surprisingly popular; the late Generalissimo Rafael Trujillo, who ran the Dominican Republic with an iron hand for three decades, was genuinely mourned by many after his assassination in 1961. Some *caudillos* have been able to pass power on to their sons, but the position requires such nerve and such a hypertrophied *don de mando* (gift for ruling) that this is rare. Such a feudal form of government is quite incompatible with a modern social structure, and it must inevitably disappear from nations that are becoming urban, developing an educated class, and being exposed to currents from outside. It survives today only in small, backward, and comparatively unimportant countries like Paraguay, Guatemala, Haiti, and Nicaragua; the last *caudillo* to control a major Latin American republic was Juan Vicente Gómez of Venezuela, who died in 1935. (The demagogic *caudillos,* like Argentina's Juan Perón and Brazil's Getulio Vargas, who appeal to labor movements, nationalism, and the demand for social reform, are a separate and transitional type.) The remaining *caudillo* regimes are all very shaky and heavily dependent on Washington. The Kennedy administration, despite the rhetoric of the Alliance for Progress, has continued arms shipments to General Alfredo Stroessner in Paraguay, renewed an agreement to maintain a Marine training mission in Francois Duvalier's Haiti, and continued to prop up the threatened regime of Luis Somoza Debayle in Nicaragua. We followed a similar shameful and shortsighted policy in Batista's Cuba, with disastrous results, but there are still people in Congress, the State Department, and the Pentagon who insist on chaining us to unpopular regimes and dying social orders. *Cau-*

y, but this kind of institutional instability makes political
ss unlikely and economic advance all but impossible.
Revolutionary Regimes. Bolivia and Cuba are the only
s in this category. Bolivia is so abysmally poor and back-
and so evidently doomed to continued poverty by her bar-
ography, that the MNR (National Revolutionary Move-
is not likely to have any great influence outside the
a plateau where it now rules. The Cuban revolution, on
er hand, taking place in a much richer and more advanced
ay, has already had an immense effect on the rest of the
here. Part of Cuba's influence is due to the initial success
evolution in raising the living standard of the farm work-
t of it to the skillful propaganda activities of the *barbu-*
arded ones), and part of it to the charismatic figure of
astro himself. "El gran Fidel" (to give him the title of a
propaganda film that was exhibited throughout Latin
in 1959 and 1960 to great applause) is a typical Hispanic
oung, handsome, energetic, brave, a superb orator and a
poet—a combination of Don Quixote, Bolívar, Trotsky,
Nicaraguan poet Rubén Darío.
pt when on their good behavior at international confer-
uba's bearded leaders have never concealed their hope
ing revolution to the rest of Latin America—and even
ited States. "The Revolution is a fountain, from which
wish may drink; the Andes must become the Sierra
f all the Americas." Such slogans reveal Castro's vision
f as a second San Martín, leading Latin America this
nst her Yankee oppressors instead of against Spanish
idea of an island nation with only seven million people
ional income about equal to what American women
cosmetics each year successfully defying the United
setting the pace for such giants as Brazil and Argen-
em ludicrous. But so did Castro's proud remark, when
ven exhausted and weaponless followers reached a
he mountains of Oriente province in 1956, that "the
[Batista] dictatorship are numbered." If revolutions
here in Latin America, *fidelismo* will be not the cause,

dillos are, after all, reliably anti-Communist and friendly to
American lobbyists, businessmen, generals, and Congressmen
with loans, grants, and sugar quotas to hand out. Every Latin
dictator except Castro received an increase in military assistance
in fiscal 1963, but not even American aid can save these outmoded regimes for very long.

2. *Conservative Regimes with Some Degree of Political De-*
mocracy. Argentina, Honduras, Ecuador, Chile, El Salvador,
Panama, and Peru fall into this category. Each has passed more
or less permanently out of the *caudillo* stage; they are ruled by
elected presidents and legislatures, and political opposition is
relatively unhampered. But political and economic power is still
in the hands of oligarchies like the "Twenty Families" of Panama
and "La Llamada" (the so-called aristocracy) of Peru. Where
half of the population is illiterate and consequently barred from
voting, or so impoverished and ignorant as not to know what
elections are about, political democracy is essentially meaningless.
In each country a small group monopolizes political and military
office, owns most of the available farmland, and fights off popular encroachments upon its power and prestige; the elite in each
of these nations has so far been able to beat back all the social
reform measures glibly promised by their representatives at conferences of the Organization of American States.

Under such conditions, politics becomes little more than a
struggle for position among a few thousand wealthy individuals,
who play a game of Hands Around with public office. If any political party with radical intentions does win an election, the
army can be relied upon to preserve the existing order. For example, in Guatemala in 1962, after a fraudulent election rigged
by Manuel Ydígoras Fuentes' official party, the army was called
out to suppress discontented students and strikers. The troops
fired into the crowds, shooting to kill; fifty demonstrators died and
hundreds more were wounded. Shortly thereafter the Peruvian
army, which had several times before nullified election victories
by the moderately leftist APRA party (American Popular Revolutionary Alliance), once again used force to bar the presidency
to its leader, Haya de la Torre. Most disheartening of all has

been the recent history of Argentina, for a long time the most advanced of all Latin American nations. As far back as the nineteenth century, in Juan Batista Alberdi and Domingo F. Sarmiento Argentina produced two great liberal statesmen; in 1916, with the victory of the Radical party in a free and honest election, the nation seemed to be firmly in the path of peaceful and democratic reform. But old weaknesses persisted; in 1930 the army once again seized power, to be followed in 1945–1955 by Perón's demagogic rule. After another free election in 1958, Arturo Frondizi betrayed his followers by surrendering completely to the Army, the Church, and the great cattle-ranch owners; and in 1962, after he made the blunder of permitting a free congressional election, he was in turn thrown out by the military. Repeated occurrences like these lend support to the argument of Ernesto "Che" Guevara, Castro's intellectual spokesman, that

Free general elections might result in new people entering the government, and they must make good their promises. . . . But the nature of the army cannot be changed without a struggle, since it is the army that has the weapons. It is bound to defend the classes doomed by history, and these will not yield without resistance.

3. *Newly-Established Liberal Regimes.* During the past decade Brazil, Colombia, Costa Rica, and Venezuela have emerged from dictatorial rule. In each case, however, the dictator left behind a legacy of waste, extravagant and unproductive public works, an empty treasury, and deepening social tensions. The fall of the dictators was accompanied by, and perhaps partially caused by, a disastrous decline in commodity prices, so that the overspecialized export economies of these nations were severely damaged. Venezuela's oil, for example, finds increasing competition from the Sahara, the Middle East, and the Soviet Union; Brazilian coffee faces the challenge of rising African production and the increased use of soluble coffees, which require fewer beans per cup; and cotton producers everywhere must cope with synthetic fabrics and the dumping of United States surpluses abroad with a subsidy of 8½ cents per pound.

The unfortunate conjunction of pol
nomic disaster has forced the newly-esta
democratic regimes to institute austerity
flation, in both cases lowering still furth
standards of their people. The largely
cated masses have come to associate
prices and hunger; this accounts for th
deposed dictators like Odría in Peru,
rón in Argentina. Democracy in these
shallow roots; civil liberties and the r
portant than a job and enough to eat.
days, when Argentines were eating tw
per capita a year, put it:

Con Perón y con Evita
La pancita es llenita.

These nations also are troubled
of the military in politics. Costa Ric
the leadership of former President J
forces still played a dominant role in
Betancourt's Venezuela, and Jänio
would have liked to reduce his
budget and institute genuine refor
refused to permit it. None of these
imitate the United States in havin
lishment and a social welfare prog
If they do not institute social ref
leftist, Castro-style uprising; if th
an officers' *coup*. Quadros ducke
Lleras and Betancourt played alo
the military, with a consequent
Brazil, Venezuela, and Argentina,
tions in the area, have suffered
bombings, and armed uprisings
elected presidents' finishing a ter

mone
progr
natio
ward,
ren g
ment)
Ande
the ot
econo
hemis
of the
ers, pa
dos (b
Fidel (
Cuban
Americ
hero—
bit of a
and the
Ex
ences, (
of expor
to the U
all who
Maestra
of himse
time aga
rule. The
and a na
spend on
States an
tina may
he and e
haven in
days of th
come else

but the catalyst and the example; as Guevara put it, "We applied certain formulas that . . . we have called discoveries of empirical medicine for the great evils of our beloved Latin America."

These new formulas—guerrilla warfare, sabotage, elimination of the regular army, a totalitarian regime, and support from the Soviet *bloc*—may seem to some Latin American intellectuals preferable to the state of things as they are. As it enters its fifth year, Cuba's revolutionary government is passing through a trying phase, trying to maintain and consolidate its power in the face of economic trouble, the absurdity of its trade relations with the Communist world, and growing internal discontent. Its future, even more than that of most revolutions, is unpredictable, for it depends largely upon decisions taken in Washington, Moscow, and Peking, and upon the mercurial temperament of Fidel Castro. But as Herbert L. Matthews put it, "We are going to have to live with Fidel Castro and all he stands for while he is alive, and with his ghost when he is dead." Castro is the first Latin American with a chance to play a significant role in world history. And if he survives and his revolution prospers, he may rank with legendary heroes like the Cid—or Lenin.

5. *Post-Revolutionary Regimes*. Mexico and Uruguay are the only Latin American nations that have passed through revolution and emerged with politically durable and relatively prosperous regimes. The revolution in Uruguay, presided over by Batlle y Ordóñez and his *Colorado* party before World War I, was peaceful, and not unlike the New Deal, which it preceded by a generation. Mexico's revolution was long and far bloodier than Castro's, and there are still outbreaks of violence on election day. But in both nations the armed forces have little political influence and in neither has there been any serious attempt at a *coup* in the past few decades.

Since other Latin nations may well follow in the path of these two, the peculiar one-party system of democracy they have evolved is noteworthy. The *Colorado* party of Uruguay ruled uninterruptedly for more than half a century; the opposing *Blancos* won an election for the first time in 1958. The Mexican

PRI (Institutional Party of the Revolution) has played an even more dominant role; it has *never* lost an election. Such a party would be considered incompatible with democracy in the United States or Western Europe, but it works fairly well in Mexico (and in India, where the Congress party plays an equivalent role). As R. A. Gomez describes it, the PRI

. . . maintains within itself the role of opposition as well as leadership, somewhat as the Democratic party does in some southern states in the United States. It has not hesitated to use the overpowering weight of government in its own behalf, but at the same time it has kept its ears well attuned to the public. It has chosen presidents who have symbolized the times—from the revolutionary Calles, to the active leftist Cárdenas, to transitional Camacho, to the businessman-lawyer Alemán, to the bureaucrat Ruiz Cortines, and finally to the labor-management mediator López Mateos. . . . These successive changes in the party leadership mirror the progress of the Mexican state from raw revolutionary leadership to the first stages of a middle-class-dominated industrial state.

In view of the long history of bad relations between Mexico and the United States, stretching from the oil expropriation controversy of 1938, back to the annexation of half Mexico's national domain after the war of 1846–1848, the present cordial state of feeling is encouraging. A quarter of a century ago the American State Department denounced Mexico's President Calles in terms reminiscent of the language used about Castro today:

An assistant secretary confided to the press that he was "morally certain . . . that a steady stream of Bolshevist propaganda [was] filtering from Mexico down through Central America, aimed at property rights and designed to undermine society and government as now constituted"—and he asked the newsmen to print the warning without involving the State Department. [Quoted in Hubert Herring, *A History of Latin America*.]

Secretary of State Frank Kellogg warned that "the Government of Mexico is on trial before the world." Yet the passage of time and the careful diplomacy of Ambassadors Dwight W. Morrow and Josephus Daniels brought about a rapprochement that led to the present mutual respect and understanding. Improbable as it seems at this writing, Castro's violently anti-American one-party rule and Kennedy's stern dictum that "Communism in this hemisphere is not negotiable" may both soften to a similar result.

Only two of the twenty Latin American republics, then, have developed stable political institutions, and it is no coincidence that these two are among the relatively prosperous. Mexico has an important middle class and a growing industrial base; her annual increase in per capita income between 1950 and 1958 was 2.7 per cent. Yet a population increase of more than 3 per cent a year puts her in the position of the Red Queen in *Through the Looking-Glass*, who had to run as fast as she could to stay in the same place. Half a century after the revolution began, as Oscar Lewis points out, "over sixty per cent of the population are still ill fed, ill clothed, and ill housed, over forty per cent are illiterate, and some forty-five per cent of the nation's children are not being schooled."

Even in Mexico, therefore, the discontent that fuels social revolutions is not altogether absent. Two other Latin nations are now passing through the destructive phases of their revolutions, with no clear picture yet of what new institutions they will build upon the ashes of the old, and in every one of the remaining sixteen a major social upheaval is either likely or at least possible in the near future. Symptoms of the approaching storm are the recurrent strikes, the occasional outbreaks of small-scale guerrilla warfare, the popularity of leftist ideologies among the intellectual classes, and the rise in anti-American sentiment which not even carefully staged presidential journeys can conceal.

The convenient classification of nations according to their political status should not lead us to expect any mechanical process of change by which each country moves predictably from one step to another. Historical prediction, despite the confident assertions of Khrushchev and Castro, is not an exact science. Inertia and habit, reinforced by machine guns, may preserve an outmoded regime long after its time is over; nations may revert for a while to an earlier stage of development; and revolutions may end in Soviet-style dictatorship, or in PRI-style democracy. But social revolutions are certainly coming, and soon. If we want to shape conditions in Latin America, we must first understand them. Toward this end, one country from each group is examined closely in the following chapters.

CHAPTER 3

The Last Caudillos: Guatemala

*Exploited by the owner of the land, the priest, the money-
lender, and the government, the Indian has been treated like
an animal, trampled upon for centuries, without more relief
than a suicidal turning to the alcohol and religion with which
they brutalize him, exploit him, and subjugate him. This is
the misery and infinite sorrow of Guatemala. When I think
of Indian villages like Chichicastenango, I choke, a shiver
runs through me.*

Luis Cardoza y Aragón,
La Revolución Guatemalteca (1955)

During the nineteenth century, while the rest of the non-
colonial nations of the world moved toward forms of representative government, Latin America remained a backwater, ruled by
whichever general retained the loyalty of the army. The history
of most nations for a century after their independence is one of
"absolutism tempered by assassination," of the meaningless rise
and fall of one Strong Man after another. With sufficient luck,
ability, and ruthlessness, such rule can be prolonged almost indefinitely; the *gaucho* Juan Manuel de Rosas controlled Argentina for a quarter of a century, Don Porfirio Díaz was President
of Mexico over a thirty-five year span, and three grotesquely
ambitious tyrants ran Paraguay for the first sixty years of its
independent existence. As recently as the 1950's a majority of
Latin America's peoples lived under a variety of one-man ruler-
ships.

But as history catches up with Latin America the old-fashioned dictators are vanishing from the scene. The paternalistic rule of the national *caudillo* and local *cacique* is as outmoded as that of the American big-city boss, and for the same reason: the governed have come to feel entitled to more benefits than the ruler is able to supply. When the Korean War ended in 1953, a dozen Latin nations, from Cuba to the Argentine Republic, were ruled by dictators. Since then the *caudillos* have been disappearing at the rate of about one every year: Brazil's Getulio Vargas in 1954, Argentina's Juan D. Perón in 1955, Peru's Manuel Odría in 1956, Columbia's Rojas Pinilla in 1957, Venezuela's Pérez Jiménez in 1958, Cuba's Fulgencio Batista in 1959, and finally the Dominican Republic's Rafael Trujillo (after three decades in power) in 1961. The trend away from this kind of government seems permanent; the greed, graft, and stifling economic climate of military rule will not long be tolerated in any nation with a growing middle class and politically conscious urban and rural workers. At the present time, only Guatemala, Haiti, Nicaragua, and Paraguay, with a total population of less than twelve million, are ruled by *caudillos*—and every one of those regimes is shaky.

It would be a mistake, however, to pass over the *caudillo* stage too hastily. For one thing, some nations may temporarily slip back under military control again, as did Argentina in the 1930's, Venezuela in 1948, Colombia and Peru in 1950, and Argentina and Peru (again) in 1962. Trujillo is dead, and Rojas Pinilla, Pérez Jiménez, and Batista so thoroughly discredited that they can never return to power. But, despite their leader's exile in Spain, Perón's followers won the 1962 Congressional elections in Argentina, provoking a subsequent military crackdown, and General Odría made a strong race for the presidency of Peru a few months later, almost winning the office through a political deal with the front-runner, Haya de la Torre. That a retired or exiled dictator can win office for a second time in a free and honest election tells us much about the novelty and weakness of the democratic tradition in Latin America.

And even after the last *caudillo's* reign is ended by evolution, revolution, or the assassin's bullet, study of the form would still be important. There will always be those who long for the strong hand of a Rosas, a Díaz, a Perón. The young men of the present generation were born and came of age under military rule; the dictators shaped their environment and their political beliefs. Even Fidel Castro, after leading a herioc fight against the brutal and corrupt Batista regime, came to resemble the deposed dictator in his personalism, his emphasis on *"machismo"* (virility), and his insistence on one-man rule. Military government may be eliminated, but it leaves its traces: after the generals come civilian *caudillos,* often with parties named after them and shaped in their image. As the marching song of Argentina's first great democratic party has it:

Adelante Radicales!	*Forward, Radicals!*
Adelante sin cesar.	*Forward without stopping.*
Viva Hipólito Irigoyen	*Long live Hipolito Irigoyen*
Y el Partido Radical.	*And the Radical Party.*

It is the party chief who comes first, and the party itself gets only the second hurrah. Habits inherited from nineteenth-century authoritarian regimes are evident even in such a stable democracy as Mexico's; the *mordida* (bribery) is endemic, no effective opposition party is permitted, and the personality of the chief executive is all-important.

Guatemala is the largest and in many ways the most important and interesting of the remaining caudilloships. Unlike Haiti, Nicaragua or Paraguay, which have never known anything but the iron hand or anarchy, Guatemala from 1944 to 1954 experienced a decade of democratic rule and the beginning of a genuine social revolution. Then, as the regime put through a radical land reform program and moved toward cooperation with the Soviet bloc, the United States financed, armed, and directed a successful invasion, and installed a pro-American dictator of the traditional type. Since that time Guatemala has received over $150 million in United States aid, more on a per capita basis than any other Latin American nation except Bolivia. The aborted revolution, the first intrusion of the Cold War into the

Caribbean, and the continued support given the present military regime by the United States make Guatemala's recent history of exceptional significance.

From 1931 to 1944 Guatemala was ruled by Jorge Ubico, a shrewd and able despot who gave the nation order and a moderate amount of economic progress in return for a share of the takings. Ruthless in dealing with political opponents (he arrested all the Communists he could catch, and executed some), he posed as a friend of the abused Indian majority and gave them promises of reform, if nothing more substantial. In October, 1944—inspired by the long-successful revolution in neighboring Mexico, by the New Deal and the Good Neighbor policy, and by the wartime crusade against fascism—middle class elements in the army, the civil service, and the university rose, expelled Ubico, and installed a liberal regime.

Juan José Arévalo, Guatemala's first democratically elected President (1945–1951), gave the country a nationalistic, progressive administration patterned after that of Mexico. A professor of philosophy who had spent fourteen years in exile in Argentina, Arévalo called himself a "spiritual socialist," and was genuinely anxious to improve the lot of the wretched Indians who made up three-fifths of the population. He abolished forced labor, encouraged the growth of labor unions, passed social security legislation, took the nation's first scientific census, began the breakup of large estates, and tried, through rural schools, cultural missions, and scholarships, to incorporate the Mayan Indians in the national life. Whatever was accomplished was done without American help; Arévalo kept out the American oil companies and rejected proffered loans because he believed that "when you take dollars with the right hand you give up sovereignty with the left."

Despite his previous lack of political experience, Arévalo showed surprising adroitness in handling enemies on the Right and the Left. He permitted the Communist Party (PGT) to reorganize in 1949 after the Ubico terror, but he did not give it juridical status, suppressed its weekly magazine *Octubre,* and sent its ablest leaders out of the country on diplomatic missions.

Arévalo avoided the error of trying to achieve too much, played the Communists, the military, the landholders, and the big foreign investors off against each other, and survived more than thirty attempted plots against him. In 1951, after six years of a remarkably successful administration, he turned his office over to his democratically-elected successor Colonel Jacobo Arbenz; it was the first peaceful transfer of power in Guatemala in half a century.

Although Arévalo had raised wages and put into effect the eight-hour day, he managed to avoid open conflict with the "Big Three" American companies that played a major role in the economy. The total investment of the United Fruit Company ($50 to $60 million), International Railways of Central America ($50 million; controlled by United Fruit until 1962); and the Guatemalan subsidiary of American & Foreign Power ($15 million) was larger than the national budget; "La Frutera" owned seven per cent of all the used arable land in the country and one-quarter of the railroad mileage. Although these companies paid higher wages than native employers and made an important contribution to the economy, they were a natural target for nationalist reformers. Even with the best of intentions, which they did not always display, United Fruit's managers could not avoid exercising enormous power; Guatemalans complained that they were "a banana republic, with the liberty of Jonah in the belly of the whale."

The thirty-nine-year-old Arbenz, determined to carry Arévalo's reforms to a conclusion, attacked United Fruit and the big native landholders head-on. Under an Agrarian Reform Law passed in 1952, five-sevenths of the company's 563,000-acre holdings were expropriated, with payment in 30-year 3 per cent bonds at the low assessed valuation of about $1.50 an acre. Those huge holdings, along with twice as much land taken from Guatemalan owners, were turned over to 100,000 Indian farm workers in one of Latin America's few major attempts at land redistribution.

This damaging blow to American investors, added to Arbenz' increasing tolerance of Communist officials in his government, called down on Guatemala the wrath of the State Department. Washington demanded payment for expropriated property at the company's valuation; Spruille Braden, a former Assistant Secretary of State for Latin American affairs, demanded armed intervention. With Dwight D. Eisenhower in office and the Good Neighbor policy replaced by the Good Partner policy, Braden's demand was answered. Secretary of State John Foster Dulles, a former member of United Fruit's law firm, brought pressure on the Arbenz regime to increase its payments to the company, to allow the entry of the American oil companies, and to take action against growing Communist influence in the labor movement and the National Agrarian Department. Meanwhile the Central Intelligence Agency began to supply Colonel Carlos Castillo Armas, an exiled officer of the Guatemalan army, with arms, airplanes, and a cash subsidy estimated at $150,000 a month.

Former CIA director Allen Dulles often complained that people did not pay attention to his agency except when it fell flat on its face. But one of the technically successful operations of which he could be quietly proud was his role in the overthrow of the Arbenz regime. While Assistant Secretary of State John Moors Cabot warned of a "focus of infection," and Senator Alexander Wiley urged action against the "dangerous beachhead of the Communist International in this hemisphere," Guatemala was effectively kept from defending herself against the coming blow. An American arms embargo had been imposed in 1948, while U. S. weapons and training missions poured into the rest of Central America; Guatemala's attempt to buy a thousand machine guns in Denmark was blocked, and a shipment from Switzerland was seized in New York in January 1954. Finally CIA agents in Europe discovered that a Swedish freighter loaded with arms from Communist-dominated Czechoslovakia was enroute to Puerto Barrios, and this was considered sufficient to prove Communist control of the Arbenz government.

Events thereafter moved swiftly. In January, John E. Peurifoy, the American ambassador in Guatemala City, announced that the United States would not "allow the establishment of a Soviet Republic between Texas and the Panama Canal," and stepped up his contacts with disgruntled officers of Guatemala's 5000-man army. In March, Secretary Dulles, who seldom showed much interest in Latin American affairs, flew to a meeting of the OAS in Caracas, and rammed through a "Declaration of Solidarity for the Preservation of the Political Integrity of the American States Against the International Communist Intervention." In May, Nicaragua broke relations with Guatemala, and Honduras expelled Guatemalan consuls from the frontier town of Copan and the seaport of Puerto Cortés. And in June, after the United States sent a confidential memorandum to all the other Latin American states, and forty-eight hours after a press conference in which President Eisenhower announced that he was "worried" about Guatemala, Colonel Castillo Armas launched his third attack against the Arbenz regime. This time he had Globemasters to fly in arms and ammunition, P-47's to bomb and strafe the capital, and enough troops to cross the Honduras border in three places and seize Puerto Barrios.

For a few days the operation was touch-and-go. Guatemala's peasants, understandably loyal to the best regime they had ever known, killed many of Castillo Armas' parachutists and recaptured Puerto Barrios. Had they been armed, and had Arbenz made an effective appeal to the United Nations, the whole American plan might have collapsed as ignominiously as the invasion of Cuba did seven years later. But Arbenz was no Castro. Under pressure from his own army chiefs, he resigned after a week of fighting, and resistance collapsed. Guatemala's new dictator, fittingly enough, made his entry into Guatemala City in a United States Air Force plane, accompanied by "pistol-packing" Peurifoy.

Arbenz and dozens of his supporters, on the other hand, took refuge behind the Iron Curtain, most of them in Czechoslovakia. Documents discovered in the deposed regime's files proved that Communist infiltration and influence in his government had indeed been considerable. While the party was legally registered only in 1952 and never had more than a few thousand members, its influence was out of all proportion to its size. Communists dominated the peasants' union (CNCG) and the central labor organization (CGTG) and affiliated them with the Communist-controlled Latin American Workers Confederation (CTAL). The president of the Guatemalan congress, the editor of the _Official Gazette,_ the Under Secretary of Education, the Deputy Director and Secretary General of the National Agrarian Department and hundreds of other officials at intermediate and lower levels were avowed Communists. Communist officials carrying out the agrarian reform distributed propaganda along with the land and as Richard N. Adams reports in _Social Change in Latin America Today:_

The program did not make the peasants the owners, but merely the tenants, of their new holdings. . . . Failure of the recipients to conform to the demands of the government, and eventually of the Communist party, would mean eviction from the long-coveted allotments.

Government-backed newspapers and the government-run radio station supported the current Stalinist line, and the expression of anti-Communist sentiments became increasingly dangerous. It may be, as former Congressman Charles O. Porter and Professor Robert Alexander believe, that "if [Arbenz] had remained in power, Guatemala would have had a post-World War II type of 'popular democracy' within six months to a year." [_The Struggle for Democracy in Latin America._]

This near-success, the first ever achieved by Soviet Communism in a noncontiguous country, underscores some of the special advantages the U.S.S.R. has in waging the Cold War in backward areas in Latin America. First of all, it has never been there before; there are no bitter memories of filibusters, interventions, racist policies, or economic penetration. Nationalist sentiment against the all-too-visible United Fruit and American & Foreign Power companies could readily be exploited by Soviet propagandists; _their_ colonial ventures are in Hungary, East Germany, etc., thousands of miles away. The U.S.S.R. can also offer aid much more rapidly and with fewer visible strings than an American president, who has Congress, public opinion, and private corporations to deal with. Finally, the U.S.S.R. offers a detailed model for rapid economic development, reflecting the glamor of proved success in transforming a peasant economy into a great industrial power.

The United States was singularly slow to comprehend the nature of the Soviet threat and woefully inept at meeting it in Guatemala. There were no pro-U.S. counterparts to the dedicated young Communist intellectuals who dominated the University of San Carlos, organized Guatemala's new labor unions, and fanned out into the hill regions to spread the gospel of Carlos Marx to the *ladinos* (those of mixed blood who speak Spanish) and the Quiché Maya. American businessmen, diplomats, technicians, and military attachés associated almost exclusively with their Latin counterparts, and too often shared the social, racial, and ideological views of the local oligarchy. Sometimes it seemed that American representatives confused the national interest with corporate balance sheets. Arévalo complains, for example, that Ambassador Richard Patterson repeatedly badgered him to open the country to the American oil companies: "For whom are you saving this petroleum?" "For Guatemala," was the proud reply; and Patterson was later expelled from the country for meddling in its internal affairs.

After our neglect had let the situation get out of hand, the "glorious victory" hailed by Secretary Dulles did for a time put an end to Communist influence in Central America. But the wisdom of our action from a long-range point of view should be questioned. For one thing, our disregard for international law weakened our moral position and the authority of the United Nations and the Organization of American States. Latin America's distrust of intervention has good grounds, and the language of the OAS Charter is unmistakably clear:

Article XV: No State or group of States has the right to intervene, directly or indirectly, whatever its motives, in the internal or external affairs of any other.

Article XVI: No State may apply or provoke coercive measures of an economic or political character to impair the sovereignty of another State.

The Eisenhower administration's return to the Bad Old Days of (lightly disguised) gunboat diplomacy set in motion a wave of fear and suspicion of the United States in Latin America that has still not subsided. Yet the State Department declared that it was Arbenz who had violated the OAS Charter by appealing to the United Nations in an inter-American dispute!

The Department further spoiled a not-very-good case by its 1957 apologia, *A Case History of Communist Penetration: Guatemala* [Department of State Publication 6465]. Preliminary declarations that Latin America was "solidly a part of the democratic world" and that the United States had "always been a bulwark of strength for the defense of the freedom, independence, and sovereign equality of the other nations of the hemisphere," could be dismissed as conventional diplomatic hypocrisy. But the document also failed to distinguish between Arévalo's genuine democratic reforms and the pro-Communist tactics of Arbenz. To the Department, the wages-and-hours and social security legislation of 1945 to 1951 were "decidedly radical," and revealed a "pro-Communist ideology." Moreover, the land reform program (which we are now urging under the Alliance for Progress) is dismissed as simply a Communist scheme to "destroy private wealth in Guatemala [and] disrupt the social and political structure and sever the links between Guatemala and the United States."

These assertions in an official government paper remind us that the Guatemalan episode took place during the closing years of the McCarthy era when anti-Communism was a ticket to political success in the United States and any social ideas more advanced than those of William McKinley were suspect. Was the Arbenz regime destroyed because of Soviet dominance—or would the United States attack as Communistic any government that expropriated American property? The State Department's simultaneous warnings against Soviet infiltration and demands for immediate payment of $16 million compensation to the United Fruit Company blurred the distinction. The CIA's high-handed operation convinced Fidel Castro and Ernesto Guevara, among others, that the United States would attempt to crush any

Latin regime that threatened American investments; Guevara was in Guatemala at the time of the invasion and offered to fight for Arbenz against the *Yanqui* State Department. The university students I taught and talked to in half a dozen Latin countries in 1959 and 1960 were still bitter about our use of "gangster tactics" (resorted to once more by a new administration against Cuba in 1961). They noted that the State Department approved of and associated itself with the Somoza and Galvez dictatorships in the invasion of Guatemala (as it used a Guatemalan air base against Cuba in 1961). Even the most convinced anti-Communist politicians and intellectuals feel that any action against Arbenz should have been a legal one, taken multilaterally through the OAS. The particular way in which we eliminated the "focus of infection" may have spread the disease elsewhere, as the immense sales of Arévalo's anti-American diatribe *The Shark and the Sardines* [English translation published 1961] suggests.

Having brought a *caudillo* into power for the first time since we installed Somoza, Trujillo, and Batista in the 1930's, the United States was in some measure responsible for his later behavior. But Castillo Armas, however important he may have been to hemispheric security and the United Fruit Company, was no blessing to Guatemala. Landlords, soldiers, employers, local bigwigs, and any conservatives with a real or fancied grievance took advantage of the restoration of the old order to settle scores; thousands were exiled, jailed, or murdered. Despite his 99 per cent majority in an election held later in 1954, Castillo Armas was thoroughly unpopular; Eisenhower spoke with conscious or (more probably) unconscious irony when he declared that "the people of Guatemala . . . have liberated themselves from the shackles of international Communist direction and reclaimed their right of self-determination." The 1945 constitution and the achievements of Arévalo were wiped out; one of the most promising social experiments in the hemisphere had been sacrificed to Communist intrigue, corporate profits, and the pressures of the Cold War.

Because of the Dulles brothers' paternal feeling for the new regime, and because it probably could not have survived without

American support, Guatemala became an exception to the Eisenhower administration's policy of making few or no loans or grants to Latin America. Between 1954 and 1962 Guatemala received more than $150 million in aid, plus the advice and assistance of many American technicians, educators, and engineers. That sum, equal to about $40 per capita, is roughly equivalent to what has now been promised under the *Alianza* to the rest of Latin America.

This infusion of dollars has not solved or attempted to solve the basic problem. The United States Operating Mission in Guatemala has done its job well, without the scandals that have marred similar programs in Bolivia and Peru; it has built hundreds of miles of new roads, all but eliminated malaria, installed clean water systems, and helped initiate self-help housing, adult education, and technical assistance in agriculture. But none of the reforms now called for under the Alliance for Progress have been attempted. In a nation where three out of four people are farmers, a few hundred owners hold more than half the land, and the average wage for farm laborers is less than 60 cents a day. Seven out of ten adults are illiterate, and half a million children (out of a total population of 3.8 million) are not able to attend school. Per capita income is only about $170 a year, and although Guatemala is the world's seventh largest coffee producer, most of her people cannot afford to drink it. Despite U. S. urging and the threat of *fidelismo*, Guatemala has neither an effective income tax nor an adequate agrarian reform program and small prospect of getting either; 1100 families still own half the nation's farm land. The regime's only "reform" bill was a law guaranteeing compensation in dollars to U.S. firms affected by expropriation or currency devaluation.

Under the Armas and Ydígoras regimes economic growth failed to keep pace with the nation's population growth of 3 per cent a year. The current net increase of 100,000 people a year has resulted in the slow erosion of an already wretchedly low standard of living. Even the wealthy planters are being squeezed; they exported 10 per cent more coffee in 1961 than the year before, but receipts fell from $78 to $68 million as a result of price declines. In October, 1962, after gold and dollar

reserves had fallen to a new low, foreign exchange controls had
to be imposed for the first time in 37 years. The small scale and
uncoordinated Alliance for Progress loans and the benefits of the
new Central American customs union did not even compensate for
the flight of capital caused by distrust of Ydígoras and his ra-
pacious cronies.

Having once experienced democracy and reform, Guatemalans are not likely to endure caudilloism and economic stagnation
very much longer. Castillo Armas was assassinated in 1957 to be
replaced, after some palace intrigues, by one of his co-conspira-
tors of 1954, General Manuel Ydígoras Fuentes. Ydígoras, who
enjoyed a salary of $12,000 a month, a Security Fund of $1 million a year, and the usual unofficial perquisites of a Latin strong
man, sensed which way the wind was blowing and made gestures toward democracy and reform. He liked to tour the countryside and distribute small gifts to the Indians, among whom he
had some of the popularity of a fatherly *cacique*. He claimed that
his only opponents were "Castro Communists," but his government was so thoroughly graft-ridden that even the big landowners
and businessmen turned against it, and he had no following at
all in Guatemala City, which dominates the rest of the nation.
In February, 1962, the chief of his secret police was murdered;
in March the army had to be called out to put down student-led
protests, strikes, and street fighting; in November rightist Air
Force units revolted and cannonaded the Presidential Palace,
narrowly missing its occupant. For the first time troops were
ordered to fire into crowds and to shoot to kill; fifty demonstrators
died, hundreds more were wounded. Finally, in March, 1963, less
than two weeks after his meeting with the other Central American
presidents and with President Kennedy in San José, Ydígoras was
thrown out of office in a typical palace revolution. The new strong
man, former Minister of Defense Colonel Enrique Peralta, dis-
solved the legislature and suspended the 1956 constitution, thus
removing the last pretense of democratic rule. Except for the
elimination of Ydígoras' grasping realtives and increased pressure
on Guatemalan reformers and *fidelistas,* the new regime will bring
about no significant changes.

Colonel Peralta's excuse for his coup, which was approved in advance by President Kennedy, was fear of the return to power of a leftist regime. Colonel Arbenz, along with José Manuel Fortuny, Secretary General of the Guatemalan Communist Party, is in exile in Havana, subsidized by Castro and making occasional propaganda broadcasts over the Cuban radio. He heads a group of several hundred Friends of Guatemala, and would like to establish a Popular Front government which would renew relations with Cuba, the U.S.S.R., and Communist China; this time, he says, "Russian rockets will protect us from invasion, as they have protected Cuba."

Arévalo, who spent much of his second period of exile teaching at the Central University of Venezuela, had announced his candidacy in 1963; it was his presence in hiding in Guatemala City that triggered the overthrow of Ydígoras. Although in his book Arévalo compared American diplomats not only to sharks, but to bandits, beasts, bullies, buzzards, criminals, drinkers of blood, gangsters, gravediggers, down through the rest of the alphabet to snakes, stranglers, thieves, whoremongers, and wolves, he insists that he prefers the Americans to Castro and Khrushchev; "Soviet imperialism is totalitarian and the other is not." Despite his antipathy to American free enterprise and his polemics against the U.S., Arévalo is an enemy of *fidelismo* as well; Cuban newspapers call him a "reactionary" and a "clown." In office, this sharp-tongued and sometimes cloudy-minded executive would have been far more difficult for the State Department to handle than the merely greedy and dishonest Ydígoras. Arévalo would once again move against the American companies and reject American diplomatic advice; there could be no more such episodes as the use of Guatemalan bases to launch the invasion of Cuba. Nevertheless, *"arévalismo"* is a legitimately democratic movement, which seems to represent the only viable alternative to a Castro-style regime. As a college professor with no army to back him, Arévalo could come to power only through elections; with its considerable influence on Guatemalan affairs, the United States could have seen to it that those elections took place as scheduled.

Once Arévalo was installed, the revolution of 1944 could have

gone forward again, this time with American support. Many of
the present useful U.S.-supported programs should continue, with
tax reforms providing the revenue to finance more of them.
Something also must be done about Guatemala's excessive dependence on coffee exports; they account for three-quarters of her
foreign exchange income, and price declines in the 1950's cost the
economy about $300 million, twice the total amount of U.S. aid.
Despite the notable accomplishments of American technicians,
sanitary conditions are appalling, especially in the ghastly slums
like "La Limonada" on the outskirts of Guatemala City. The death
rate from diarrhea is 270 per 100,000; Guatemala has the highest
child mortality rate in Central America and an average life expectancy of less than forty years. In rural areas, there is only one
doctor for every 100,000 people. The nation needs everything:
doctors, sewage systems, schools, housing, roads, farm machinery,
rural electrification, port facilities, and technical aid of every kind.
Most of all it needs a reform government like Arevalo's, but
American preference for a military regime makes an honest election impossible.

The Kennedy administration has so far been unwilling to apply
the rhetoric of the Alliance for Progress to the Guatemalan situation; Ydígoras and Peralta may be scoundrels, but they are *our*
scoundrels, and provide a reliably anti-Castro voice and vote in
the OAS. Colonel Peralta has asked for $85 million in *Alianza*
money, and will probably get a large part of it. But propping up a
fading caudilloship, as our experience in Batista's Cuba shows, is
an expensive, unpopular, and in the long run impossible, task. We
are still asking the Guatemalan military to behave and shipping in
the arms with which they murder civilians; military assistance to
the regime was doubled in fiscal 1962–1963. If we persist in talking about reform yet trying to fight against the rising demand for
political and economic change, we will foment desperation which
could produce another *fidelista* regime in Guatemala, this one
with land borders and ports on both oceans.

CHAPTER 4

Peru: A Conservative "Democracy"

So far no party nor candidate has arisen willing to take responsibility for the steps which would bring an end to the Peru as it is now known. But it is only a matter of time before someone appears—visionary or demagogue, it will not make a great deal of difference—who will organize the power of five million Indians for his own ends. Then, not all the rifles of the civil guard, the tanks of the army, the destroyers of the navy, or the jets of the air force, will be able to resist a reform which will be more akin to revolution.

    Richard W. Patch,

"A Note on Bolivia and Peru,"

American Universities Field Service Reports, *IX, No. 4* (*April, 1962*)

With caudilloship and direct military rule on the way out, many Latin American nations moved during the 1950's to a more advanced political stage. As the decade ended, three Central American states (El Salvador, Honduras, and Panama) and four South American ones (Argentina, Ecuador, Chile, and Peru) had come to enjoy a considerable amount of political democracy, with civil liberties, competing parties, and elected presidents. But in none of the seven was political democracy effectively translated into social reform and economic progress. Everywhere the old ruling classes retained their privileges, turning the political process into what Castro calls "an electoral farce." Behind the elected president in all these countries stood the Army, usually allied with the oligarchy and prepared to defend it by force if

42

necessary. Democracy's roots were so shallow in these nations that Peru and Argentina, the two largest, slid back under military control in 1962 after elections which failed to please the generals. The history of Peru over the last few decades reveals with particular clarity the inherent instability and ineffectiveness of Latin America's conservative democracies.

An analysis of Peru must begin with a description of its enduring geographic problems—problems that resemble those of several other Latin nations. The country is divided into three sharply contrasted regions. The smallest but most important of these is the coastal lowland, a strip ranging in width from ten to sixty miles wedged between the sea and the maritime *cordillera* of the Andes. The area's climate is dominated by the cold Humboldt Current and its accompanying blanket of cool air; temperatures are mild, relatively unchanging, and there is little or no rain all the year round. Ninety per cent of the region is bleak, sterile desert; the other 10 per cent, along the fifty or more rivers coming down from the mountains, is splendidly fertile under irrigation, and produces export surpluses of sugar and cotton. Substantially all of Peru's petroleum comes from the far northern desert, or from offshore wells. Guano, a rich natural fertilizer, is collected from rocky headlands and islands to the south. Lima, the capital, with a metropolitan population of over 1.7 million people, is located in one of the fertile river valleys near the sea.

In this coastal region of severely restricted arable land, concentration of ownership has reached levels unusual even for Latin America. One hacienda alone is one-third the size of Cuba, and eighty plantations, with a total of nearly nine million acres, comprise almost half of the farm area; 35,000 small farmers, with an average of five acres each, own less than one-fifth as much. Worse off even than the peasants are the farm laborers, who must often work three or four days a week for the right to cultivate a tiny plot of the hacienda's poorest land. Lima itself presents even sharper contrasts of great wealth and grinding poverty. In the old aristocratic quarters of the town, and in the gleaming new suburbs near the sea, *Limeño* society still lives in a way that reminds the visitor of the *douceur de la vie* of the Old Regime in France. But the slums on the northern side of the river Rimac, across from the Lima that the tourists see, are as bad as any in the continent. Ten or twelve people live in a single room; there is endemic tuberculosis and venereal disease, and a daily diet of 1200–1500 calories, barely above the starvation level. Per capita income on the coast is about $120, but social conditions are far worse than this low figure would suggest. Lima, for example, has over 100 churches, many of them lavishly endowed— but three out of five slum babies die in infancy, and there is only one children's hospital in the city.

Highland Peru, with a third of the nation's land area and three-fifths of its population, plays only a minor role in the economy. Most of the Indian inhabitants of the region, scattered in remote Andean valleys or concentrated in the Callejón de Huaylas, have not changed their way of life since the Conquest; they scratch out a bare existence from their fields of corn, wheat, and potatoes, and their flocks of sheep, llamas, and alpacas, and they hardly enter the money economy at all. Twelve hundred landlords own *seventeen million acres*, a staggering 80 per cent of all the arable land in the *sierra*, while 20,000 peasant families own only three-quarters of 1 per cent; some of their plots are measured not in acres but in furrows or square meters. The overwhelming majority of the Indians own no land at all, work half of each week for absentee owners, raise miserable crops on the poor soil, are treated like serfs, and live like animals. Except for the huge foreign-owned open-pit copper mines at Cerro de Pasco and Toquepala, there is little development and there is no connection with the rest of the world. In the *sierra*, the pangs of hunger are ever-present, dulled only by *chicha* (native beer) and the narcotic coca leaves; a survey carried out by the University of Ayacucho showed that only 2 per cent of the people in that district had the annual income of $250 that is considered necessary for a "minimum decent standard of life."

The third and least important region is the *montaña*, the tropical rain forest east of the Andes. This green wilderness, inhabited only by scattered primitive tribes, experienced a thirty-year boom before World War I, when the price of natural rubber touched $3 a pound. But competition from Asian plantation rubber and, later, synthetics, has caused it to revert to jungle, and it now contains only 5 per cent of Peru's population. As the economic potential of the coast and the *sierra* is so sharply limited, the *montaña*, remote and hard to conquer as it is, holds whatever future the Republic has. Four centuries of failure to develop the region should serve to caution us against undue optimism.

These three sharply-differentiated and inhospitable Peruvian regions are typical of all the countries lying across Latin America's mountainous backbone. Like the others, Peru is heavily dependent on foreign trade (nearly one-quarter of the gross national product was exported in 1961), although she is fortunate in having a variety of commodities to export rather than just one or two. Sugar and high-quality long-staple cotton head the list; frozen and canned fish and fish meal have become important items in the last few years. (Peru is now the world's largest fish meal producer, accounting for 30 per cent of output and 50 per cent of world exports.) Petroleum and its derivatives have been significant, but annual production has been static for some time, and home consumption is rising. The remaining exports are metallic minerals: large amounts of lead, copper, and zinc, and smaller quantities of silver, gold, and vanadium.

During World War II, under the moderate administration of President Manuel Prado, foreign investors and land owners prospered as a result of satisfactory prices and stable demand for all of these products. American money poured in to increase production of rubber, quinine, and metals, and to insure Peru's loyalty to the Allies. But prosperity, as in the United States in the 1920's, put off the undertaking of much-needed reforms; few benefits trickled down to the millions of *cholos* (mixed breeds) and Indians at the wide bottom of the social pyramid. "*La llamada,*" the aristocracy of a few hundred families of pure Spanish blood, lived in Lima or abroad, and took no interest in the welfare of their *peones*. The oil fields and the lead, zinc, and copper mines were foreign-owned and lightly taxed; wartime profits went mostly to American stockholders. Political uncer-

tainties and the instability of the *sol* encouraged native and
foreign capitalists in Peru (as everywhere in Latin America) to
invest their surplus abroad. Despite its backwardness and poverty-stricken economy, Peru was actually exporting capital to
the United States.

At the end of the war the APRA, the long-outlawed left-
wing party of Indians, *cholos,* mulattoes, and young intellectuals,
came to power as part of a new democratic coalition. The APRA,
founded in 1923, took its program from the successful Mexican
revolution: labor and social security legislation, land reform, and
heavy taxation or expropriation of foreign mining properties.
After suffering exile, jail, torture, and death for most of two
decades, the *Apristas* were in no mood to be gentle with their
enemies; strong-arm squads administered beatings to political
opponents, and were blamed for the murder of two conservative
newspaper publishers. There was a series of politically inspired
strikes; exports dropped, and the exchange rate fell drastically.
After the failure of an APRA-prompted revolt in the port city of
Callao in 1948, General Manuel Odría seized dictatorial power
with a bloodless *coup,* and kept it for the next eight years.

The Odría dictatorship was an unusually mild one. He jailed
several hundred *Aprista* leaders, and hounded others out of the
country (the six-year imprisonment of APRA's founder, Haya de
la Torre, in the Colombian Embassy in Lima was an international
cause célèbre), but in Peru there was none of the demagogy,
mob violence, and police brutality that marked the contemporary
dictatorships in Argentina, Brazil, and Venezuela. A calm, un-
ostentatious professional soldier, General Odría quietly intro-
duced a series of useful social reforms. He built elementary
schools in the Indian villages of the highlands, and provided
teachers who gave instruction in Quechua, the native language.
He won labor union support by permitting moderate pay rises
and providing hospital insurance and pensions. He freed foreign
trade and investment of all incumbrances, and attracted new ,
capital to Peruvian mining and manufacturing. Finally, to every-
one's astonishment, he permitted an almost free election in 1956,
left the country before the ballots were counted, and permitted

the chosen successor to be defeated. With APRA support, conservative Manuel Prado was elected to a second term.

Odría, like Calvin Coolidge, left office just in time; as he went into voluntary exile in the United States, world prices for Peru's exports went into a decline that has not yet ended. Sugar dropped from 5 cents a pound in 1956 to 3 cents in 1962; in the same period zinc fell from 13 to 11 cents; copper from 41 to 31 cents; lead from 15 to 10 cents. These catastrophic declines cost the nation tens of millions of dollars in desperately needed foreign exchange; at the same time the essentials that Peru must import—foodstuffs, medicine, machinery, mining and farm equipment—increased in price.

The United States, which had been friendly to the Odría dictatorship (he was given government loans, surplus foodstuffs, two submarines, three destroyers, and the Legion of Merit), appeared to the Peruvians to be downright hostile to the democratic government that succeeded him. Yielding to small but politically powerful pressure groups, President Eisenhower took a series of steps that seriously damaged Peru's shaky economy. The United States refused to sponsor or join commodity stabilization agreements on anything but wheat (which we export) and sugar (which was subject to a quota giving favored treatment to the Batista and Trujillo dictatorships). In July, 1957, in order to protect high-cost domestic crude oil producers, the United States put into effect a program of "voluntary" import quotas; these were made mandatory in March, 1959. In mid-1958 the suspended duty of 1.7 cents per pound on copper was restored, and later the same year new import quotas on lead and zinc were imposed. At the same time, surplus cotton held by the United States under the farm price support laws was dumped abroad with a subsidy of 8 cents a pound, taking away traditional Peruvian markets. American fishing interests continued to violate Peruvian coastal waters, and tried, unsuccessfully this time, to get a prohibitive tariff placed upon Peruvian tuna. Measures such as these had the appearance of commercial warfare waged by a very powerful nation against a weak one, though this was unintentional, and they were a main cause for the stones, saliva, and insults showered on Vice-President Nixon when he visited Lima in 1958.

Even the elements seemed hostile to Peru's emerging new democracy. For two years the rains failed in the highland valleys of southern Peru: crops withered, hundreds of thousands of cattle had to be slaughtered, and one million subsistence farmers had to be rescued from famine. (U. S. emergency relief in the area was marred by bi-national incompetence and corruption; 60 per cent of the grain shipped in was wasted or improperly sold, and some of it was fed to cavalry horses.) Shortly afterward the Humboldt Current mysteriously moved out to sea, taking with it the marine life that thrives in its cold waters. Half the adult guano-producing birds died, three million fledglings were found dead, and millions of eggs rotted away unhatched. The production of guano was cut in half; the government had to ration farmers and raised the price to sugar cane, cotton, and coffee producers from $18 to $80 a ton, thus increasing the cost of production at the very time that all three of these crops were menaced by falling world prices and America's restrictive trade practices. In January, 1960, as a finishing blow, one of the severest earthquakes in many years struck Arequipa, Peru's second largest city, causing heavy loss of life and extensive property damage.

These repeated economic, political, and climatic blows brought the underdeveloped Peruvian economy to the edge of disaster. Foreign exchange reserves vanished, the foreign trade deficit steadily widened, and the national budget deficit climbed to 880 million *soles* in 1958 and 1 billion *soles* in 1959. Inflation, which Peru had avoided while the currencies of her neighbors came crashing down, finally overtook the *sol*, which dropped from 19 to the dollar in 1957 to 31 to the dollar in June, 1959. Next month, in desperation, President Prado dismissed his Finance Minister and called in Pedro Beltrán, a wealthy plantation owner, banker, and editor of Peru's most important newspaper, *La Prensa*, and gave him full powers over the economic life of the nation.

Beltrán, whom *Fortune* magazine hailed as a "providential one-man earthquake" and "a new elemental force in the Americas," put into effect the orthodox austerity measures recommended by our State Department. Increased tariffs, quotas, and credit restrictions cut imports by one-sixth for the full year 1959; aided by a small recovery in commodity prices, Peru turned a trade deficit of $60 million in 1958 into a $26 million surplus in 1961. Beltrán increased the government's income without raising taxes (there is still no export tax on minerals, such as Chile passed decades ago) by tightening collection procedures; the big corporations were put on a pay-as-you-go basis, required to pay disputed items first and submit a claim for repayment later. A generous Industrial Promotion law provided special tax exemptions and duty-free imports to new investments, and government expenses were cut by eliminating subsidies that had held down food prices. With this splendid Free Enterprise record behind him, Beltrán was even able to pry loans out of Robert Anderson, Eisenhower's chilly Secretary of the Treasury; he got $53 million by his warning "You've lost Cuba to Castro already. How much more are you prepared to throw away?"

The resulting business statistics looked good. The government's improved cash position permitted advance repayment of an International Monetary Fund loan, and the *sol* recovered to 27.5 to the dollar and remained steady. With a balanced budget, freely convertible currency, and price increases for the Standard Oil Company and International Telephone and Telegraph Corporation monopolies, Peru's investment climate was attractive, and hundreds of millions of dollars flowed into dozens of small manufacturing plants, exploratory oil drilling along the south coast and in the Amazon, iron mines at Marcona and Acari, and the gigantic open-pit copper mine at Toquepala, 11,000 feet up in the Andes. For a time Beltrán thought his record would enable him to win the presidency in 1962; he formed a new *Independiente* party and resigned from the cabinet to be eligible to run. But he soon found out that his program was not nearly as popular in his own country as it was in Wall Street and in the

Luce publications; as he himself sadly announced, "I am the most hated man in Peru." In the end he did not even file his candidacy.

Beltrán's was, in fact, a banker's prosperity, from which only the *hacendados* and the foreign companies benefited. Economic growth continued to lag behind the booming population increase of 3 per cent a year, so that per capita income actually *fell* 2.7 per cent between 1958 and 1961. Civil liberties and democracy meant nothing to the Indian farm laborer (who could not vote anyway, since he was illiterate); all he knew was that every year he had less to hope for and less to eat. In 1961 and 1962 half-starved bands of *comuneros* (communal landholders) began to arm themselves with pickaxes, shovels, and shotguns, and attempted to seize plantations in the *sierra*. Beltrán and Prado had the uprisings bloodily suppressed, and blamed the troubles on Cuban agents and "Communist infiltration from nearby Bolivia." The accusation is partly true; I have myself seen Cuban agents at work in the Communist stronghold of Cuzco and the University of San Marcos in Lima, and met Peruvian "exchange students" taking lessons in guerrilla war in Havana. But Peru's conservative regime was doing nothing to forestall these agents of revolution with genuine reforms of its own.

To begin with, Beltrán's land reform program, produced after four years of study by a commission headed by a lawyer for the Cerro de Pasco corporation, would not affect the 3500 *hacendados* who own two-thirds of the nation's arable land. Maximum holdings were set at 625 acres (1250 acres for pasture land), limits which a careful student, Professor Richard W. Patch, calls "far too generous to conform to the realities of population pressure." Furthermore, the program would not apply to any estates formed before the law went into operation—a stipulation that reduced the plan to an absurdity. Provision for a minimum wage and a guarantee of the right to organize rural labor unions were eliminated from the measure. The desperate problems of Peru's landless farmers were to be solved by settling them in the trackless *montaña,* an impractical scheme which even its authors admit will take forty years to complete, without taking population increases into account. (It is no coincidence that Beltrán and his associates own sugar plantations in the area of proposed colonization.) Peru clearly does not have that much time. Yet the Kennedy administration was willing to accept these "reforms" (which were only proposed and not enacted) as honest coin, exchangeable during the *Alianza's* first year for $66 million in grants and loans.

Housing was the other half of Beltrán's much publicized plan for "*Techo y tierra*" (a roof and land). There is a shortage of some two million decent dwelling units in the *sierra* and in the city slums; in Lima tens of thousands are literally living on top of a garbage heap (*el montón de la basura*). But the government program does not even keep up with the *barriadas* (shanty towns) pushing out into the desert on the outskirts of every coastal city, and does nothing at all to improve the miserable mud huts of the mountain villages. Furthermore, the privileged classes take a share of the inadequate program that exists. Hundreds of low-cost government-built houses are assigned to army officers, who need no subsidy, and the Inter-American Development Bank's first $1.5 million housing loan went to the Peruvian Portland Cement Company—in which the Prado family has a controlling interest. American private enterprise has also entered the housing field with ideas represented by the following description from *The New York Times* (July 1, 1962):

The International Basic Economy Corporation has announced plans for the immediate construction of 800 *low-cost* [italics mine] housing units on the outskirts of Lima. The corporation was founded by Nelson Rockefeller to help raise living standards in underdevolped areas. . . . The homes will be sold for $3,000 to $5,000 [several times the lifetime earnings of the average Peruvian] with a thirty per cent down payment. . . . The houses will have exterior and interior gardens, servants' patios and service entrances, combination living and dining rooms, bedrooms, baths and kitchens.

Such a grotesque "solution" to the housing problem would be comic if existing conditions were not so desperate.

A third area in which Prado and Beltrán were unable or unwilling to make needed reforms was in the reduction of the military budget. Peru's old border disputes with Chile and Ecuador have never been settled definitively, and the political influence of the armed forces in all three countries is such that they command a substantial part of the national budget (14 per cent in Chile, 21 per cent in the other two). In November, 1960, in response to an overture from Chilean President Arturo Allesandri, President Prado expressed himself in favor of a disarmament conference that would end the "fruitless and burdensome" arms race; but his sincerity was called in question when, two weeks later, he announced the purchase of two six-inch-gun British cruisers, the *Ceylon* and the *Newfoundland* (now the *Almirante Grau* and the *Coronel Bolognesi*) for the Peruvian navy. Peru is still paying for the squadron of Canberra bombers purchased from Britain some time ago and for four modern, snorkel-equipped submarines bought in the United States by Odría for $8 million each. Peruvians themselves joke about having "the best protected fish meal fleet in the world," but no president would dare to deprive the armed forces of their expensive toys. The United States must take part of the blame for fomenting this foolish arms race among nations that can so ill afford it, nations that have not fought a war of any kind for over eighty years. Between 1945 and 1960 the U.S. supplied Peru with $53 million for "hemispheric defense," making this the second largest program of its kind in Latin America; in fiscal 1962–1963, despite the premises of the Alliance for Progress, military grants to Peru were almost doubled.

The hollowness of democracy and the continuing hold of the military upon Peru were revealed with striking clarity during and after the 1962 presidential elections. With Beltrán voluntarily out of the race, the three leading candidates—the APRA's Haya de la Torre, Fernando Belaunde Terry of the Popular Action Party, and General Odría with his personal following—campaigned upon essentially similar moderate reform anti-Communist programs. Anxious to avoid a military *coup*, all three denounced *fidelismo* and all carefully extolled the armed forces and promised them new pay raises and privileges. Yet when no candidate received the one-third of the votes required for victory (Haya came in first with the other two not very far behind), the Army stepped in, annulled the elections as "fraudulent," and installed a military junta to rule by decree, "in order to preserve democracy." Symbolically enough, a U.S.-supplied Sherman tank broke down the gates of the Pizarro palace, and the officer who led the assault and arrested seventy-two-year-old President Prado was Colonel Gonzalo Briceño, a graduate of the U.S. Ranger school at Fort Benning, Georgia. (Army Chief Nicolas Lindley Lopez, one of the Junta's members, had received the U.S. Legion of Merit in 1961 for his "consistent support of democratic principles.")

Despite its fairly good record on political and civil liberties, then, the Prado-Beltrán regime undertook no significant social reforms and did not break the military stranglehold upon Peruvian democracy. It seems clear that under Peru's existing system of rule by the Army, the Church, and "la llamada," no real benefits will be brought to the depressed masses. The same must be said for all seven nations in this category, which together contain one-fourth of Latin America's area and population. Uruguay is the only Latin nation where social reforms have been brought about peacefully and democratically; everywhere else the ruling classes have refused to yield their privileges except in the face of armed revolts (as in Mexico, Bolivia, and Cuba). The other countries in Peru's situation have at least experienced some significant social movements in the past, such as the Radical and Peronist periods in Argentina. Peru is almost unique among the nations of the world in never having known a successful social upheaval; the country is like France before 1789, and there are no immediate signs of any assault upon the Bastille.

But the same conditions that led to the Mexican revolution, to the MNR (National Revolutionary Movement) uprising in Bolivia, to *peronismo* in Argentina and *fidelismo* in Cuba, are present in Peru—a lopsided export economy, a shortsighted oligarchy of landowners, generals, churchmen, and foreign investors, a growing number of city workers living in abject misery, and a substantial body of farmers living outside the money economy altogether. The new *Junta,* which has jailed hundreds of so-called "plotters against stability," is only a caretaker regime, able to do little more than mark time. If the ruling classes continue to refuse to come to grips with the nation's problems, they will be swept out of power by force.

In dealing with transitional regimes of this conservative type, the Kennedy administration has been as hesitant and contradictory as in handling the remaining caudilloships. While none of them has passed the tax and land reform programs called for by the *Alianza,* all have received *Alianza* loans and grants. In its anxiety to ward off disorder and *fidelismo,* the administration went so far as to continue Alliance aid to the generals who overthrew constitutional government in Argentina and imprisoned President Frondizi in April, 1962. Yet when Peru's generals carried out exactly the same kind of *cuartelazo* (barracks revolt) three months later, Kennedy responded by temporarily cutting off all aid and breaking diplomatic relations; no wonder the generals were astonished and angry. On August 17, the first anniversary of the Alliance for Progress, the United States changed its mind and renewed relations and Alliance aid to the *Junta.* American policy had once again been ill-judged and inconsistent, and the Latin military were reassured that they need not fear American reaction to *coups* and *cuartelazos.*

It was Cuba's (and Argentina's) Ernesto Guevara, once again, who predicted just such military vetoes of the popular will. In a speech in Peiping in November, 1960, he declared that:

We know from our experiences in Cuba that the Army is part of the oligarchy, and serves the oligarchy, and will defend the oligarchy. Therefore, political measures are of no value. . . . Our Latin American friends cannot match the beautiful realities achieved in Cuba . . . through ballot boxes, nor through an underground opposition, nor through winning parliamentary seats by cleverly maneuvering—as in hypocritical Latin American democracies. It is through armed struggle of the people sharply directed against the opposition clique. It is through arming the people and smashing the puppet dictatorial regime that a people's army supplants the latter regime.

If the oligarchy continues to block reforms in countries like Peru and Argentina, revolutions will certainly follow—and soon. The peasant leader, Hugo Blanco, already dominates a growing area around Cuzco where national control does not exist, and where he is putting into effect an Agrarian Reform program of his own. Some conservative democracies may indeed be able to evolve peacefully, along Uruguayan or New Deal lines. But the United States had better be prepared with alternative policies in the event that money, moral suasion, and the menace of *fidelismo* do not frighten the elite in these conservative pseudo-democracies into effective social reform.

CHAPTER 5

A Liberal Democracy:
Betancourt's Venezuela

We have a firm, well-defined line in international policy and in economic policy. Just as we protested to the U. S. State Department over the U. S. purchase of sugar from the dictatorship of Santo Domingo, so . . . we sent a note of protest to the Cuban Government when Major Guevara . . . said that we Venezuelans should go like people approaching the Jordan to receive a revolutionary baptism, alongside him and his co-militants. And we said to him that the people of Venezuela overthrew their tyrant, the people of Venezuela held elections, and the people of Venezuela built up their institutions without receiving foreign advice or entreating anyone to lend them crutches with which to walk along their path.

Rómulo Betancourt (1960)

The Alliance for Progress, President Kennedy's ten-year plan for economic aid to Latin America, has the merit of emphasizing the need for social reform as a necessary condition for economic growth. The area's archaic and unjust systems of taxation and land tenancy, as the President tactfully but firmly pointed out, must be modified if the underprivileged masses in those countries are to enjoy the benefits of modern technology. Aid under the program will therefore be channeled to those nations that are prepared to change the feudal characteristics of their society, so

56

that our assistance does not continue to make the rich richer and
leave the poor as wretched as before.

Despite the President's gratifying sophistication about economic aid and his fine rhetoric about "a vast effort, unparalleled
in magnitude and nobility of purpose," it remains to be seen if
his policies measure up to Latin American realities and aspirations. For the first time in our history we are threatened by a
rival ideology in this hemisphere; Fidel Castro's Cuba has already abandoned democracy and capitalism to experiment with
the Soviet system of dictatorship and state ownership and control. If Castro survives and achieves some measure of success
with his headlong course, the much less spectacular Kennedy
Plan may seem too slow to Latin America's awakening masses
and the intellectuals who lead them; a number of Castro-like
governments might seize power. A crucial test of our policies will
come in Venezuela, Cuba's Caribbean neighbor, the richest nation in Latin America, governed by a liberal leader but still
plagued with typical economic and social problems.

In the years that have elapsed since the overthrow of a military government in 1958, Venezuela's democracy has barely managed to survive a series of attacks by forces of both the left and
right. Throughout 1962 a series of riots, and bus burnings, two
insurrections by disgruntled Marine officers, and a leftist attempt
to seize Caracas made it seem that the country might be about
to slide back into some form of dictatorship. To retain control,
Betancourt has repeatedly had to close the schools, censor or
shut newspapers, ban political meetings, jail hundreds of his opponents, and—an embarrassing step for a former revolutionary—
call in the army and place the entire country under martial law.
Some reports of torture and "suicides" in government prisons are
as bad as anything that occurred under the Batista or Jiménez
dictatorships.

These disorders have been accompanied and intensified by
continued signs of economic distress. The construction business
is in a severe slump, and exploration and drilling programs in
the crucial oil industry are running at about half their 1959 lev-

els. Even with dollar revenues of more than $100 million a month, the current budget has a $250 million deficit; $100 million in foreign capital was taken out of the country in 1962, and in the past three years Venezuela's dollar reserves have fallen by more than $1 billion. Despite Betancourt's promise that a $200 million loan from fifteen U. S. banks was the last his government would make, he is again looking for foreign assistance, and has had to devalue the bolívar, once one of the world's hardest currencies.

These continued deficits and disorders are particularly discouraging because of Venezuela's large and varied resources and the honest, able, and patient leadership of Rómulo Betancourt. If liberal democratic reforms do not work here, they are not likely to be successful in less richly endowed Latin American states. Venezuela, unlike some of its Caribbean neighbors, is not overpopulated; its population of less than 7 million occupies an area one and one-half times as large as Texas, and only 3 per cent of its land area is at present under cultivation. There is a substantial cattle industry (the country has more cows than people), considerable production of such varied crops as coffee, cacao, rice, sugar, corn, and potatoes, and a remarkable variety of mineral resources. In the Guiana Highlands south of the Orinoco, which contain half the area of the country but only 3 per cent of its population, there are still largely unexploited reserves of asbestos, bauxite, coal, diamonds, and so on down to uranium. The current production of iron ore from the same area's immense reserves feeds a small domestic steel industry and makes Venezuela the largest ore exporter in the world. Dwarfing all these activities is the oil industry, whose output of 3.3 million barrels a day makes the nation the third largest producer in the world (after the United States and the Soviet Union) and by far the largest exporter. Oil furnishes 90 per cent of Venezuela's exports, brings the government revenues of more than $3 million a day, and is responsible for the country's per capita income of more than $800, the largest in Latin America. With such resources to draw from, economic difficulties should be no more than temporary.

Some of the problems facing the Betancourt regime are indeed short-term, dating back from the 1948–1958 dictatorship of Marcos Pérez Jiménez. Like most Latin dictators, "PJ" stole large amounts of money and wasted still more. He left behind him $1.2 billion in promissory notes and such expensive mementos as an uneconomic $400 million steel plant, a railroad with hardly any freight or passengers, a money-losing government airline, an incredibly lavish Officers' Club and the magnificent (but generally empty) Hotel Humboldt, perched on a 4,000-foot hill overlooking the capital. These white elephants have caused much of the current pressure on the bolívar.

A more serious difficulty, for a country so heavily dependent on a single commodity for export, is the current world oil glut, increasing competition from the U.S.S.R., and the closing of certain outlets for Venezuelan crude oil. Proved reserves in the Soviet Union have risen to 60 trillion barrels, the current output of about three million barrels a day is scheduled to grow to nearly twice that by 1965, and consumption, owing to the shortage of Soviet automobiles, will remain comparatively low. Cut-rate Soviet oil has been finding purchasers in half a dozen Latin-American countries, and in Finland, Denmark, Sweden, Italy, West Germany, Ceylon, India and Pakistan as well, so that all the international producers have had to lower prices to meet the competition. When Fidel Castro seized the Standard, Shell and Texaco refineries in Cuba, the whole of that small but significant market was lost to Venezuela. Argentina, which imported $300 million of oil a few years ago is now almost self-sufficient, and even exports small quantities, and the Eisenhower-Kennedy quotas on United States oil imports have also damaged Venezuelan prospects. As a result of these and other factors, Venezeula exported 30 million more barrels in 1960 than in 1959, yet received 56 million bolivares less in income. The government's 70 per cent share of oil profits fell from $823 million in 1958 to $740 million in 1960.

Betancourt, who is only the second democratically elected president of Venezuela (the first, novelist Romulo Gallegos, was ousted by a junta of army officers and wealthy landlords in 1948), is of course not responsible for the current economic mess.

Having come to power just when the slump started, however, he is blamed for it in the same way that Herbert Hoover was held responsible for the crash in 1929. Agricultural workers and unemployed slum-dwellers remember that they were a little better off economically, in the booming times of Pérez Jiménez (and the Suez oil crisis); "PJ's" ouster brought back civil liberties, but these have now been taken away again, prices continue to climb, and jobs are harder to find than ever. It is not surprising that many of the 100,000 unemployed *caraquenos* eagerly listen to *Prensa Latina's* glowing accounts of how well things are going in Cuba, and have come to agree with Fidel Castro's attacks on parliamentary democracy as only another disguise for exploitation of the working class.

The smoldering discontent that lies so close beneath the surface of Venezuelan life is most readily apparent in Caracas, where a quarter of a million people live in slums as bad as any in South America. In the past fifteen years the capital's population has shot up from 700,000 to 1.3 million, which is one-fifth of the nation's total. Every day since 1959 an average of one hundred families has moved into the slums, worsening already desperate shortages of housing, schools, hospitals, electric power, transport, and water supply. One sees in Caracas the meaninglessness of per capita income figures; it is quite misleading to strike an average between the bureaucrat or businessman living in a gleaming luxury apartment house and the unemployed laborer living in a hut made of packing cases and corrugated iron, without electricity or running water. Such contrasts are sharper in Caracas than anywhere in Latin America. The windows of the splendid Officer's Club, for example, look out on a hillside scabbed over with wretched hovels, from which in the rainy season tons of human excrement wash down. Caracas has more cars per hundred people than any other Latin American city, and traffic jams as bad as those in Detroit or Los Angeles. The visitor is impressed by the Octopus, a new elevated highway connecting the different sections of town and perhaps more impressed when he looks beneath it, and finds thousands of poor squatters using the road as a roof. The capital is the only area Betancourt and his Democratic Action (AD) party failed to carry in the 1958 elections, and they received less than one-fifth of the vote there. Many of the workers who seized arms when Pérez Jiménez fled still have them, and there is strong *fidelista* sentiment among the politically important student groups at the university; only the army's heavy hand keeps order.

The social situation out in the countryside is just as lopsided and unstable. A 1957 survey showed that some 4000 landowners, less than 2 per cent of the proprietors of farms, held about four-fifths of all the cultivated land in the country. Two-thirds of all the farms were smaller than thirteen acres, and 14 per cent were less than three acres. Some 350,000 rural families, nearly a third of the total population, were without any land at all. The 40 per cent of the population that lives off the land produces only 7 per cent of the gross domestic product, and the country cannot feed itself: wheat, dried milk, meat, potatoes, and even eggs are imported from the United States, and some lettuce is flown in from as far away as Holland. Farming methods are generally primitive, and much of the land is so poor that in some places corn, for example, yields only two bushels to the acre, as compared to 40 bushels in the United States. Already inadequate living standards are threatened by a population increase of 3.6 per cent a year, as against an economic growth rate of only 1.4 per cent in 1960 and 1961.

These grave social problems are of course nothing new. Venezuela's masses have always been poor, dirty, landless, hungry, and illiterate; what has changed is their former willingness to endure such conditions as part of the natural order of things. The well-named "revolution of rising expectations," kindled by the sight of luxuries close at hand and fanned to a blaze by propaganda emanating from Moscow, Peiping, Havana —and Hollywood—is as strong in the Caracas slums as in any underdeveloped area in the world. Despite his government's economic difficulties, Betancourt is doing what he can in the way of land reform, housing programs, and increased educational opportunities. The difficulty is that expectation outruns achievement, and opposition parties can always promise more than the government in power is able to deliver.

As is usual in Latin America, the cutting edge of discontent is provided by the students. The armed groups that fortified the Pharmacy School and defied the police in 1960 showed the source of their ideology by nicknaming their strongest positions "Stalingrad" and "Sierra Maestra." They are supported by the radical Republican Democratic (URD) Party, which quit the government coalition in 1960, by the Communists, who got 6 per cent (160,000) of the Congressional votes in 1958, and by the ARS group and the Movement of the Revolutionary Left (MIR), *fidelista* splinters of the AD. Late in 1962, after a wave of terrorist holdups and sabotage, the MIR and the Communist Party were declared illegal and some of their deputies arrested. On the other flank Betancourt has been (at times literally) under fire from officers involuntarily retired in 1958, disgruntled captains and colonels on active duty who long for the return of military rule, and occasional assassins hired by Pérez Jiménez or by Generalissimo Rafael Leonidas Trujillo of the Dominican Republic.

The troublesome and dangerous job of dealing with these almost overwhelming internal difficulties is complicated by the increasingly tense international situation in the Caribbean. Dictatorships of the left and right feel themselves menaced by Betancourt's middle-of-the-road regime, and Venezuela's president still bears the scars caused by a dynamite explosion arranged by Trujillo in 1960. This attempt on the life of their freely elected ruler by a hated despot naturally brought a wave of sympathy in Betancourt's favor, and strengthened his position. The appeal to violence emanating from Havana is more pervasive and more dangerous. Cuba's economic problems—monoculture, the *latifundio* (large landed estate), and dependence on the U.S. market and capital investments—are so similar to Venezuela's that Castro's radical solutions naturally have a considerable appeal to Venezuelan students, labor union leaders, and left-wing politicians. The social and economic program of the Cuban revolution, its achievements suitably touched up for export, are constantly reiterated by Cuban "tourists," diplomats and the *Prensa Latina* radio station. Before Betancourt barred Cuban emissaries and the Venezuelan police shot the leader of the 26th of July Movement in Caracas, Castro spent more money in Venezuela than anywhere else. In Havana in 1961 and 1962 I met oil workers and union leaders from the Lake Maracaibo region who had been invited by the Cuban government for revolutionary holidays or indoctrination courses. They were impressed by the farm cooperatives they had seen and were violently in favor of the revolution. "If the Yankees ever attack Cuba," one of them said to me, "we will blow up every one of their wells in Venezeula." During the Cuban missile crisis of 1962 some of them tried to do just that, and for a few days shut down 600 Creole wells producing one-sixth of the nation's output of crude oil.

Betancourt's struggle against *fidelismo* was not helped by the shortsighted policies of the Dulles-Herter State Department and the blundering incompetence of those Congressmen and Senators from Mississippi and Louisiana who play such key roles in shaping our Latin-American policy. Venezuelans remember that Pérez Jiménez received United States armaments, loans, and the Legion of Merit, the highest award that can be given to a foreign citizen; nobody in Washington objected to "PJ's" tyranny or incredible waste and graft, so long as he met his obligations to New York bankers and cooperated with Standard Oil, Mobil, Gulf, Texaco, and the other oil companies. During his years of exile Betancourt had to swallow numerous slights from American officials eager to remain on good terms with the dictator, and the restoration of democratic government was greeted by some of those officials with the sour comment that "the investment climate in Venezuela has rapidly worsened."

The United States moves against the revolutionary Cuban regime have also been managed with little regard for the awkward position in which they placed Venezuela. In June, 1960, for example, the Venezuelan Labor Federation (CTV) and several URD leaders pledged themselves to support the Cuban revolution against its "*Yanqui*" enemies. The United States delegation at San José that August, however, insisted on a strong anti-Castro stand, a step which most Latin American governments would have preferred to avoid. Angel Luis Arcaya, Betancourt's URD foreign minister and chief of the Venezuelan delegation to San José, fought for a milder resolution; when beaten, he refused to sign the final declaration, and on his return to Caracas he was greeted as a hero. Betancourt's dismissal of Arcaya, followed by the resignation of all the URD cabinet members, led to student riots mentioned above. Senators Ellender of Louisiana and Eastland of Mississippi did not help matters when they declared that "what Latin America needs is more dictators like Trujillo" and "wished there was a Trujillo in every country in Central and South America." Shortly afterward, Trujillo was given 322,000 tons of the sugar quota taken away from Cuba. Our diplomatic "triumph" at San José left Castro as strongly in power as ever and achieved nothing but the weakening of an invaluable ally.

In the meanwhile, the streets of Caracas, still heavily guarded by troops equipped with tear-gas bombs and machine guns, are quiet. The leftist opposition has evidently decided that Betancourt cannot be overthrown by a popular revolution just now, and that a more patient policy is indicated. The government's repressive measures, they believe, will be a continuing source of resentment, and in the long run they do not think Betancourt's moderate reform program will satisfy popular aspirations. The success or failure of these programs during the next few years will determine the political future of Venezuela, and it is in implementing them that Betancourt is running into a number of obstacles.

A major and seemingly ineradicable difficulty is the continued dominance of the military in Venezuelan public life, and the generals' habit of regarding themselves as a kind of super-legislature. Betancourt remembers quite well that his mentor Gallegos was thrown out of office when the army decided that it did not like his land and tax reforms, and he therefore treats the opinions of the defense minister, General Antonio Briceño Livares, with great caution and respect. The army's loyalty, moreover, must be paid for. Betancourt is obliged to do continual obeisance to the "important role" of the military as "the advance guard for the defense of our sovereignty," and to spend a quarter of his budget on the practically autonomous armed forces. Even so, the 150-year-old habit of conspiracy continues. No elected president has ever finished out his term in Venezuela, and if Betancourt is unlucky or makes a major missstep, the army will send him to join his unfortunate predecessors.

The government's land reform program has also had to be carried out very slowly, and in such a way as not to interfere with any vested interests. Venezuela has never had a tax on land, and Betancourt does not dare to impose one. The Agrarian Reform law does not touch privately-owned estates that are under cultivation, and it guarantees payment in full for whatever land is expropriated. One plantation in Portuguesa State, for example, was purchased for $480,000 and turned over to some three hundred farm families, who also had to be given loans for seed, equipment, and living expenses. Other farmers have been settled on formerly unused government lands, which require expensive penetration roads and irrigation projects. According to a survey made by the Farmer's Federation (which strongly backed Betancourt in the 1959 elections), at the end of 1961 only 12,000 families had received land, and the total area granted was only 750,-000 acres. As Congressman Selden of Alabama pointed out after a visit to Venezuela, resettlement of all the landless rural families at the present rate will take at least fifteen years and cost about $7 billion. Venezuela does not have that much money, and may not have that much time to head off a social revolution. Mild as it is, the agrarian program is bitterly resented by the landholding oligarchs, who see themselves losing their supply of cheap labor and their old status as feudal lords.

Industrializing the nation, the dream of every Latin American government, also presents grave problems. Venezuela is one of the highest cost countries in the world, perhaps the only one whose citizens fly to Miami or New York for an "inexpensive" vacation. Under their new contract the oil workers will receive $23 a day in wages and fringe benefits, so that it is more expensive to hire a man in Venezuela than in Texas or California. These high costs have edged Venezuelan crude oil out of several markets, and make it quite impossible for manufacturers to find an overseas outlet. As a result, Venezuela has had to protect her infant industries with high tariff walls, and to stay outside the developing South American Common Market. But the home market of 6.6 million people, nine-tenths of them bitterly impoverished, cannot support any sizable industrial plant. Betancourt has recently chartered a government industrial corporation which he hopes will make "a second Ruhr" of the Orinoco Valley, but even the officials in charge admit that it will take decades to turn their ambitious blueprints into reality.

The government programs in education and housing are also handicapped by prior commitments and lack of funds. During his first two years in office Betancourt built schools for some 90,000 pupils and provided free lunches for some 100,000 poor children. But one-quarter of the population remains illiterate, and tens of thousands of students are still without classrooms. Fidel Castro's Cuba, with infinitely smaller resources, and at the cost of a social civil war, has done more. Illiteracy in Cuba was all but eliminated by a massive education-and-indoctrination program in 1961. The Venezuelan housing program also lags behind Cuba's. Less than 20,000 low cost houses have so far been built, and, just as in Peru, a scandalously large number of them have been set aside for officers' families, who certainly do not need additional subsidies.

Since the government cannot cut the army's budget and is unwilling or unable to impose land or income taxes, the only way to speed up these programs would be to draw greater revenue from the oil companies. As previously noted, however, the present state of the world market for oil is discouraging. Betancourt's decision not to grant any more concessions has brought new investment to a halt, yet the government oil company formed in 1960 is too small and slow-moving to take up the slack. Officials of the company were not even appointed until a year after its incorporation, and its production at the beginning of 1963 was only 20,000 barrels a day (as against 1.2 million a day for Creole, a subsidiary of Standard Oil). The company seems to have been established merely as a sop to the nationalist groups who have been demanding a Castro-like expropriation of foreign-owned properties.

The resignation in March, 1961, of the finance minister, Dr. Thomas Enrique Carillo Batalla, after only three months in office, was a sign of renewed financial crisis. Dr. Carillo's orthodox program, aimed at balancing the budget and halting the flight of capital, depended upon a $900 million long-term loan from Washington, a sum vastly in excess of anything the United States was willing to grant. The collapse of his minister's ambitious plans meant still another setback for Betancourt's hope of reviving Venezuela's economy and financing liberal reforms.

Despite his difficulties Betancourt is, of course, sympathetic to the Kennedy program; his comment upon it was that "the White House begins to speak a language that has not been heard since the days of Franklin Delano Roosevelt." Venezuela's president is an old personal friend of A. A. Berle, for a time Kennedy's chief adviser on Latin American affairs. Betancourt was also highly satisfied with the appointment of Teodoro Moscoso, first as our ambassador to Venezuela, and then as head of the Alliance for Progress. Moscoso, former head of "Operation Bootstrap" and the first Puerto Rican appointed to ambassadorial rank, speaks Spanish as his native language and has an exceptional grasp of Latin American economic problems.

Despite these promising auguries of understanding and good will, Kennedy too must reckon with internal political factors that may adversely affect his Latin American program. It is going to be very hard to persuade Congress to provide more money for loans to nations that have squandered so many billions already; Representative Otto Passman of Louisiana, whose subcommittee passes on foreign aid appropriations, has a long record of successfully cutting down such programs. Venezuela's mineral exports to this country are also under pressure. When Arthur Goldberg, then our Secretary of Labor, visited Hibbing, Minnesota, to investigate unemployment there, for example, he was told that "charity begins at home," and asked what the government intended to do about curbing iron ore imports. President Kennedy has also continued the quota on oil imports. West Virginia coal miners and United States oil producers, unlike Venezuelans, can vote and make campaign contributions, and powerful Congressmen and Senators from these areas must be placated. Such pressures may force further cutbacks and delays in a program that seems somewhat inadequate to begin with, and the Venezuelan people may not be willing to wait.

The nation's troubles will probably be intensified by the approach of the Presidential elections scheduled for December, 1963. Betancourt, with his decades of political experience, his prestige among Venezuela's three million peasants, and his devotion to democratic reforms, will be difficult to replace. He was able to remain in office longer than any other elected President by inaugurating some genuine reforms, by retaining the loyalty of the army, and by being tough enough to crush rightist and leftist uprisings. As he rounds out his last year, he can look back on varied achievements: the completion of the five-mile, $80 million bridge over Lake Maracaibo, the opening of the government steel plant at San Tomé de Guayana, the building of many roads, hospitals, and aqueducts, the inauguration of a functioning (if slow-moving) agrarian reform program, the reduction of illiteracy from 57 per cent in 1958 to 27 per cent in 1962 and the enrollment of 118,000 new pupils in the school year 1961–1962 alone. But the major economic problems—landless farmers, 400,-000 unemployed workers, and half the nation's wealth going to only 12 per cent of the income earners—remain. The real measure of Betancourt's accomplishment will come in 1963–1964, when it will be seen if he can supervise an honest election and turn power over peacefully to his successor—something that has never happened in all Venezuela's history.

The consequences of a lapse into political instability would be very serious. After the 1962 coups in Argentina and Peru, a military dictatorship in Venezuela must still be considered a real possibility, though it is doubtful if it could endure very long. If democratic reform does fail, the nation might well take a sharp turn toward Castroism, and a Fidel Castro in Caracas would make even our troubles with Cuba look petty. Cuban sugar is not, after all, an essential commodity, and because Cuba

is an island she can be effectively isolated by the United States
Navy operating out of our bases on the mainland and at Guantan-
amo. But Venezuela supplies a substantial part of the Western
Hemisphere's oil, and two-fifths of United States iron ore imports;
United States businessmen have $3.5 billion invested in the coun-
try, three times their former stake in Cuba. Despite a sharp drop
in *fidelismo's* appeal after the missile-and-bomber crisis of 1962
and Cuban-sponsored sabotage of American properties in Venezuela, Castro retains some following among students, farm
laborers who have not yet received land, a few dissatisfied junior
army officers, and the nation's 15 per cent unemployed urban
workers. Fabricio Ojeda, a former URD congressman, has spent
many months in Havana as a guest of the revolutionary government, and is an honorary lieutenant in the Cuban army; Cuba set
aside the week of November 5–12, 1962 as one "of solidarity with
the brave guerrilla warriors of Venezuela." While all such revolts
launched so far have fizzled out, the nation's mountain regions
are ideal for Castrolike operations, and her land frontiers border
the most impoverished and rebellious regions of Brazil and
Colombia. These dark perspectives may seem rather remote. But
no Latin American nation has yet achieved genuine social reform and stability without a revolutionary upheaval; after ob-
serving Fidel Castro's headlong rush toward Communism we cannot ignore the possibility that the same thing may happen in
liberal democracies such as Venezuela, Colombia, and Brazil, all
of which suffer the same social ills that bedeviled pre-1958 Cuba.

Cuba: A Revolutionary Regime

Fidel Castro is part of the legacy of Bolívar, who led his men over the Andes Mountains, vowing "war to the death" against Spanish rule, saying, "Where a goat can pass, so can an army." Castro is also part of the frustration of that earlier revolution which won its war against Spain but left largely untouched the indigenous feudal order.

Senator John F. Kennedy,
The Strategy of Peace (1960)

The most serious of many ways to misunderstand the Cuban Revolution would be to regard it as an aberration, as an irrational bolt from the blue conceived and carried to triumph by one megalomaniacal young man with a beard. It is true that Fidel Castro's powerful but erratic personality shaped the successful guerrilla war against the Batista dictatorship, and has played a key role in the subsequent course of the new revolutionary regime. But the Cuban upheaval, as Senator Kennedy understood, has its roots in the Hispanic-American past; there have been revolutions like it in Mexico and Bolivia and there will be similar uprisings elsewhere, no matter what happens to Castro himself. We must learn to understand and to deal with these coming revolutions as natural, and perhaps inevitable, accompaniments of the transition to a modern political and social order.

Even the briefest survey of recent Cuban history must begin with a few words about the island's tragic and endlessly frus-

trated past. Called by Columbus "the fairest island human eyes
have yet beheld," Cuba in the sixteenth century speedily became the scene of oppression and horror. The peaceful and hos-
pitable Taíno Indians, enslaved, forced to work beyond their
strength in the mines, whipped, tortured, hunted down with
bloodhounds, were all but exterminated within a few decades.
The Negro slaves who were brought in to replace them were not
much better treated; the first recorded slave revolt, bloodily suppressed, occurred as early as 1533. But the Negroes and the in-
stitution of slavery survived, to become a principal obstacle to
Cuba's later efforts to win freedom from Spanish control.

The unsuccessful resistance of the Indians under their chief
Hatuey, and the abortive slave revolt of 1533 were only the first
of many uprisings against Cuba's masters. The revolt of the *ve-
gueros* (planters) against the tobacco monopoly in 1717–1723,
the independence conspiracy organized by Román de la Luz in
1809–1810, the Negro uprisings of 1812, the José Francisco Le-
mus underground organization of 1821–1823, the attempted slave
revolt in Matanzas in 1844, the Narciso López filibustering ex-
peditions of 1850 and 1851 were all mercilessly crushed. During
the *Guerra Grande,* or Ten Years War (1868–1878), the Spanish
commander gave orders that anyone caught aiding the revolution, and "every doctor, lawyer, notary, or schoolteacher captured with the insurrectionaries, should be immediately shot";
the war cost some 200,000 lives and caused $700 million in prop-
erty damages without achieving the island's independence. The
bitterness of these struggles, and the long delay in bringing about
reforms (even slavery was not abolished until 1886) help explain
the violence of the social revolution when it came at last in 1959.

When Cuba finally did achieve her freedom from Spain in
1898, she did so only to pass into the control of another foreign
power. The United States army ruled the island directly until
1902; thereafter, under the Platt Amendment to the Cuban constitution, Cuba consented to American intervention "for the preservation of Cuban independence, the maintenance of a government adequate for the protection of life, property, and individual
liberty." The United States exercised this right directly in 1906–

1909, when Theodore Roosevelt sent a Nebraska lawyer to govern the island, and again in 1917, when marines were landed in Camagüey and Oriente Provinces to protect American sugar, mining, and railroad properties. Throughout the 1920's the mere threat of intervention made the use of armed force unnecessary; the United States sent unofficial advisers to Havana with the understanding that their advice would be followed—or else.

Direct American rule, under John Brooke (1899), Leonard Wood (1899–1902), and Charles Magoon (1906–1909), was at least reasonably honest and efficient. Cuban self-government, operating under the shadow of the Platt Amendment and American economic domination of the island, veered from the cheerful grafting of Presidents José Miguel Gómez (1909–1913), García Menocal (1913–1921), and Alfredo Zayas y Alfonso (1921–1925) to the monumental brutality and dishonesty of Gerardo Machado y Morales (1925–1933). The United States seemed satisfied as long as succeeding regimes paid their debts, protected American investments, and were properly subservient to the American ambassador in Havana; on a list of desirable characteristics for a Cuban president to possess drawn up by Sumner Welles in 1921, the first and last points were "his thorough acquaintance with the desires of this Government [and] his amenability to suggestions or advice which might be made to him by the American Legation."

Machado evidently met these qualifications. When he planned to extend the presidential term from four to six years and have himself reelected, he went to Washington and secured Coolidge's blessing in advance. American businessmen were so satisfied with a dictator who expelled "labor agitators" and put corporate interests before his country's that Thomas Lamont of the banking firm of J. P. Morgan publicly expressed a wish that Machado could be kept in office "indefinitely." Only in May, 1933, when economic troubles and growing terrorism made it clear that the dictatorship could no longer maintain order, was Sumner Welles sent to Havana to help arrange a transition to a more stable regime.

Encouraged by tacit American support, opposition elements

stepped up their activities; in August, after a brief general strike, Machado fled the country. Unfortunately, from the State Department's point of view, the change of governments threatened to become a real revolution. In September an uprising of army non-commissioned officers headed by Sergeant-stenographer Fulgencio Batista y Zaldívar overthrew the docile interim regime and installed a new one "whose theories," Welles reported in alarm, "are frankly communistic." Provisional President Ramón Grau San Martín, a former professor of biology at the University of Havana, promptly justified these fears by passing a minimum wage law, cutting the rates paid to the electricity company owned by United States interests, and abrogating the Platt Amendment.

During the brief term of the Grau government, Welles and his successor Jefferson Caffery bombarded Washington with reports of its radicalism and inability to keep order. Recognition of the regime was withheld and thirty warships, including the battleships *Mississippi* and *Wyoming*, were sent to Cuban waters. When Grau managed to keep order despite these pressures, Welles dismissed his accomplishment: "Where quiet prevails, it is the quiet of panic." Ambassador Caffery agreed with Welles as to "the inefficiency, ineptitude, and unpopularity with all the better classes in the country of the *de facto* government. It is supported only by the army and ignorant masses who have been misled by utopian promises." Democracy and a New Deal were all right for the United States; Cuba was not to be allowed to have either.

American interference naturally undermined the civilian regime's position and resulted in continued fighting and disorder. In a key interview early in October, Welles told Batista that "in my judgment he was the only individual who represented authority in Cuba. I added that this was owing, in part . . . to the determined and decided action of the troops against Communist and radical elements. That fact . . . had brought to his support the great majority of the commercial and financial interests of Cuba." Suitably encouraged, Batista threw his lot in with the Americans and ousted Grau on January 15, 1934; recognition followed within a week.

For the next ten years Batista ran Cuba by a shrewd combination of force, demagogic promises of reform, and solid friendships with American businessmen and diplomats. The old army hierarchy had been eliminated by the time he came to power; every one of the new officers owed him personal allegiance. He rewarded them and the enlisted men by pay raises, splendid uniforms, clubhouses, playing fields, and generous pensions. Organized labor was kept in line by the government-controlled Confederation of Cuban Workers (CTC), while newspapermen and student leaders were brought around by the distribution of "bottles" (well-paid sinecures). Improved sugar prices and wartime prosperity permitted Batista to give the island a government better than any it had ever known. For Cubans on the inside, for American tourists, diplomats, and businessmen, Cuba was a low-cost tropical paradise.

Not far from the tourist hotels and the beautiful beaches, however, was another Cuba which few visiting Americans ever saw—the Cuba of the Havana slums, the sugar *centrales,* and the mountain regions of Oriente Province. This was the Cuba where only one child in three attended school, where some 25 per cent of the population was unemployed except during the brief sugar harvest, where hundreds of thousands of families had to survive somehow on incomes of less than $200 a year, where shoes, toilets, electricity, and even meat, milk, and vegetables were luxuries. As A. A. Berle summarized the situation, the prosperous war years meant only "great luxury for a relatively small group in Havana and a small rise above the starvation level for the masses." The Cuban *guajiro* uncomplainingly accepted his lot; the angry young men at the university had to choose between silence and prison, exile, or execution.

By 1944 Batista had temporarily had enough. He permitted a free election in which Grau San Martín was returned to office and then retired to Miami with a fortune estimated at $40 million. It didn't take Grau long to succumb to temptation; he was indicted by his successor, Carlos Prío Socarrás, for misappropriating $178 million during his administration, but escaped conviction when gunmen stole the pertinent documents before his trial. Prío in turn distinguished himself by building a $2 million home on a salary of $25,000 a year, and by appropriating $20 million in worn-out paper money that had been turned in to be destroyed. The average Cuban accepted corruption as fatalistically as a citizen of Jersey City under Boss Hague; political life was so demoralized that honest men sometimes pretended to be receiving graft, lest they be looked down on as stupid.

But Prío made the mistake of permitting Batista to return to Cuba. The army's allegiance to the pudgy ex-sergeant had never wavered, and on March 10, 1952, several months before the scheduled elections, Batista brought off his second *coup*. Once again every solider in the ranks became a privileged being, and every officer's commission a license to steal. Seventeen of Havana's eighteen newspapers were on the government payroll. Only a few editors, like Jorge Zayas of *Avance*, were clumsy enough to accept checks. Most of them, along with a number of United States newsmen and Florida police chiefs, took cash. Under Eusebio Mujal the CTC became an efficient damper of labor discontent and a source of additional graft. Student leaders at the university (*"el bonche"*) were again bought off with "bottles" or funds from *"el baga."* For the discontented the regime kept in reserve Decree Law 997 on Public Order and the brutally persuasive methods of the Military Intelligence Service (SIM).

Both the Batista dictatorship and the corrupt civilian regimes that had preceded it provided what the State Department liked to call "a favorable investment climate." American companies controlled 40 per cent of the island's sugar lands, 80 per cent of its public utilities, 90 per cent of the mines and cattle ranches, and, in combination with Shell, substantially all the oil business. American investments in Cuba ran to more than $1 billion, equal to over one-third of Cuba's gross national product, and Cuba's 6.5 million people were our sixth best customer, dependent on us for everything from razor blades to bulldozers. With the island's economy booming, all these interests prospered, and our diplomacy reflected the State Department's equation of "freedom" with "free enterprise." Arthur Gardner, the American ambassador in Havana from 1953 to 1957, especially devoted himself to the interests of the Cuban Telephone Company, and managed to secure a big increase in rates. He was so effusive in his praise that he embarrassed even the dictator: "I'm glad Ambassador Gardner approves of my government," Batista remarked, "but I wish he wouldn't talk about it so much." Earl E. T. Smith, who succeeded Gardner, was also a businessman, inexperienced in diplomacy and Latin American affairs, whose primary qualification for the appointment seems to have been his work as finance chairman of the Republican Party State Committee in Florida in 1955. With Batista holding power by naked terror, and with the bodies of his opponents frequently found sprawled in the streets, Smith devoted himself to "business as usual"; he appeared to accept Batista's promises about civil liberty and free elections at face value, and Washington apparently accepted the ambassador's views on Cuba.

The boldest of the dictator's opponents was a young Havana lawyer, Fidel Castro. A graduate of Havana University, Castro had already taken part in an abortive attack on the Trujillo dictatorship of the Dominican Republic in 1947, and had participated in the anti-U.S. riots in Bogotá in 1948. A month after Batista's 1952 *coup*, the twenty-six-year-old lawyer submitted a brief declaring the dictator's assumption of power unconstitutional and demanding prison terms against him totaling 100 years. The brief was, of course, rejected, and Castro turned to conspiracy. On July 26, 1953, the date that was to become the title of his movement, he led 170 young men in a foolhardy assault on the Moncada army barracks in Santiago de Cuba, in his native Oriente province. The revolt was drowned in blood, Batista's troops killing some of the seventy prisoners they took by castrating them and letting them bleed to death. Castro and his twenty-year-old brother Raúl were captured in the Sierra Maetra hills and escaped being killed only by a series of lucky accidents. At his trial before the Urgency Court that October, Castro acted as his own attorney. In a remarkable five-hour summation, published in English under the title *History Will Absolve*

Me, he defiantly admitted his leadership of the uprising, and outlined the comprehensive plan of social and political reform for
Cuba that he would have put into effect had the revolt succeeded.

Sentenced to fifteen years' imprisonment, Fidel and Raúl
actually served nineteen months in the Boniato penitentiary on
the Isle of Pines and then were released under a general am-
nesty. They left immediately for Mexico, where other exiles of
the 26th of July Movement were waiting for them. It was in
Mexico that they met Ernesto "Che" Guevara, the young Argentine physician who was to become a brilliant guerrilla leader and
the chief Marxist theoretician of their movement. On December
2, 1956, after harrowing misadventures, they put a force of
eighty men ashore near a small fishing village in Oriente. Their
yacht, the *Granma*, went aground, and they had to abandon their
painfully collected radio transmitters, arms, ammunition, food,
and medical supplies. Coordinated uprisings elsewhere in the
island were crushed; pursued by U.S.-trained and equipped
regular troops, and bombed and strafed by U.S.-built aircraft,
only Fidel, Raúl, Guevara, and a handful of others escaped to a
hideaway in the mountains. It was many months before this nucleus collected enough men to begin guerrilla operations.

Other groups meanwhile launched attacks of their own
against Batista. In Matanzas province there was an unsuccessful
Castro-style assault on the Goicuría barracks; in Havana a group
of students headed by José A. Echevarría briefly seized the radio station and the presidential palace, but failed to find Batista
and were hunted down, tortured, and shot. The army and the
police were by this time understandably jittery, and ready to kill
on mere suspicion. To be young in those days was to be suspect,
and to be a university student was enough in many cases to war-
rant a sentence of death. Hundreds of mangled bodies were left
hanging from lamp posts or dumped in the streets in a grotesque
variation of the Spanish colonial practice of public executions.
All told, Batista's second dictatorship cost the Cuban people
some 20,000 dead.

By the end of 1957 Castro's operations in the Sierra were in full swing, with hundreds of peasants and young men from the cities buying or stealing rifles and joining the rebels. The bearded guerillas blew up bridges and trains, burned cane fields, and made lightning raids on army posts to secure supplies. Theodore Draper's argument that the uprising was "essentially a middle-class revolution" ignores the key roles played in it by rural and urban workers, especially in Oriente province. Serving as guides in the trackless Sierra, providing food, shelter, and clothing, reporting the approach of government troops, and (in small numbers) joining the ranks of the rebel army, they made it possible for the revolt to survive and grow strong. The leaders of the movement, to be sure, were middle class, and generally well-educated, and it has support and financial help from some of the middle and upper classes; even the well-to-do could no longer stomach the increasing corruption and brutality of the regime. Batista's 46,000-man army, supported only by favored politicians, labor leaders, businessmen, landowners, and the American Embassy, was engaged in an open civil war.

After his first visit to the Sierra, in February, 1957, Herbert L. Matthews of *The New York Times* correctly predicted that Batista "ought to be able to hang on for the nearly two years of his present term [but that he could not] possibly hope to suppress the Castro revolt." American diplomats and military men were far slower in deciphering the handwriting on the wall. Ambassador Earl E. T. Smith tried to persuade Homer Bigart of the *Times* not to go to the Sierra because Castro was "just a Communist with a small band of thieves and robbers." In November, 1957, U. S. Air Force Major General Truman H. Landon flew into Havana to award the Legion of Merit to Colonel Carlos Tabernilla of the Cuban Air Force, who had directed an air attack on the city of Cienfuegos several weeks before. During the same month Marine Corps General Lemuel C. Shepherd publicly toasted Batista as "a great general [and] a great president." In December, 1958, less than a month before Batista's fall, Senator Allen J. Ellender of Louisiana gave a press conference in Havana in which he urged that arms shipments to the Cuban government be resumed:

Of course, I don't know much about it, but if a nation requires weapons to maintain internal security, I personally cannot understand why they should not be shipped. . . . People on the Washington level evidently feel that the shipment of weapons to the Cuban government under the circumstances might be picked up by Russia for propaganda purposes. But I do not think this is valid. It would be a tragedy for Cuba if civil war were to take place here. The poor people would be the ones to suffer. And Cuba is too prosperous and too wonderful a little island for such a thing to happen.

Asked if he thought Cuba was in a state of civil war, Ellender cautiously replied, "I don't know of any. Has there been any fighting?"

By March, 1958, when the Pentagon had reluctantly cancelled further arms shipments, Batista's troops had had all the equipment they would have needed to defeat the few hundred men then in the Sierra—if they had known how to use it. During the preceding two years our "modest" shipments to Cuba under the Mutual Security Program included 3000 rifles, 15,000 hand grenades, 4000 rockets, 7 tanks, and a battery of mountain howitzers costing $330,000. Even after the arms shipments were halted, an American military mission remained in Cuba, actively assisting Batista's army. In a letter to President Eisenhower dated August 26, 1958, José Miró Cardona, who then as in 1961 represented the Cuban exiles in Miami, asked that these missions be withdrawn, as it was "obvious that they train and support the armed forces of the dictatorship." The State Department thought it over for seven weeks, and then explained that withdrawal of the missions in case of a civil war was "permissive rather than mandatory," and that "hemispheric defense needs" required the United States to continue training Batista's men. Our officers remained to the very end; they were on hand at Camp Columbia when Castro's victorious *barbudos* rolled in to take over. When I visited the city of Santa Clara in 1960 I was shown the marks of the bombardment by B-26 airplanes on December 28–31, 1958, and a bomb fragment marked with a handshake and the words:

Mutual Defense
MADE IN U. S. A.

Given this record of United States assistance to the Batista dictatorship and our support of previous Cuban dictatorships, it is easy to understand why Castro came to power suspicious of American intentions toward him. "The tyranny," he told his followers, "unquestionably counted on the support of the United States . . . Batista managed to keep his troops in action for so long by telling them that he had U.S. backing." Able American critics of Castro such as Draper and Professor Frank Tannenbaum are agreed that our sorry and shameful policies between 1952 and 1958 were largely responsible for the emergence of Castro-style Communism in Cuba. As Teresa Casuso, a Cuban delegate to the United Nations when she broke with the regime in 1960, wrote in *Cuba and Castro*:

Fidel would have won much more quickly if Batista had not had the moral and material support of the United States. With a shorter war, the figure of Fidel Castro would very likely never have swelled to the gigantic dimensions which it acquired in proportion as the Cuban people suffered and despaired. Fidel was only one of the factors in our national life. It was not necessary for him to be made into a god, and the master of the whole country. Once again, the United States is paying the price of its short-sightedness.

Despite some signs of coming trouble, however, Cuban-American relations were reasonably good during the early months of 1959. Castro's first cabinet was made up of well-to-do, moderate men, newspaper owners, lawyers, engineers, an architect, a judge. Batista's friend Earl Smith was recalled, to be replaced (although only after a month's delay) by Philip W. Bonsal, a capable career diplomat with the valuable experience of dealing with the Bolivian revolution behind him. "I am under the impression," Castro declared after learning of Smith's recall, "that the United States is changing its attitude toward Cuba and will remove the things that caused friction [in the past] but that is for the United States to say." The regime's public trials and executions of Batista police and army officers were bitterly (and at least in part unfairly) criticized by American newspapers, Congressmen, and Senators, and Castro characteristically replied to their threats in kind. But he almost immediately withdrew and apologized for his offhand remark about "200,000 gringos" dying on the beaches if the United States should send Marines. [W. A. Williams, *The United States, Cuba, and Castro* (1962) corrects the misleading account of this incident given in Tad Szulc and Karl E. Mayer, *The Cuban Invasion* (1962).]

After the uproar over the so-called "blood-baths" died down, Castro made a reasonably successful unofficial visit to the United States in April, invited by the American Society of Newspaper Editors. He frightened American security officials by plunging into the midst of excited crowds, and puzzled Washington by talking to people he met in the streets, as if he were a candidate for office. But he made a good impression on the editors who had invited him, and on the members of the Senate Foreign Relations Committee with whom he talked in a closed session. The important question of Cuba's future relations with the United States was not dealt with, however. Felipe Pazos, Castro's National Bank president, and Rufo López Fresquet, his Minister of Finance, have both testified that Castro "expressly prohibited" them from speaking about loans. In private, however, Fidel was "quite candid" about his need for American aid, and in a speech in Buenos Aires a few weeks later he outlined a ten-year $30 million program for Latin America along the lines of what later became the Alliance for Progress.

But the Eisenhower administration was not interested in financing social revolutions. Treasury Secretary Anderson and the officials of the International Monetary Fund were willing to lend money to countries such as Argentina, Bolivia, and Chile provided they agreed to welcome American private capital and to accept stabilization programs that had the effect of bearing down heavily on the lower classes. But they were not prepared to furnish Castro the money he needed to develop the Cuban economy on terms that he was willing to accept. Confident that Cuba's economic dependence on the United States would soon bring the new regime to its senses, American officials decided to sit back and await developments. Vice-President Nixon went further; in a memorandum written after a conversation with Castro, he recommended that a Cuban invasion force be recruited, trained, equipped, and put ashore to eliminate a regime that would be dangerous to American business and security on the island.

With Castro's suggested scheme for massive United States aid ridiculed by American officials, he proceeded to reshape the Cuban economy on his own. Soon after his return from Buenos Aires he made clear what he had meant when he told cheering crowds in Havana that "the Revolution has not yet ended in Cuba; it has just begun." On May 17, 1959, at his old headquarters in the Sierra Maestra, he signed the Agrarian Reform Law, and with it began the transformation of the social structure of the Cuban countryside. The provisions of the law were, in appearance, moderate; Castro claimed his government was "only trying to move from feudalism to enlightened capitalism." Private landlords were permitted to keep 1000 acres of land, or 3300 acres in land devoted to cane, rice, or cattle. In view of the fertility of Cuba's soil, and the fact that crops can be grown all year round, these are generous limits. Larger estates (*latifundios*) were to be expropriated, leaving the owner a nucleus of 1000 acres, with payment made in 20-year 4.5 per cent bonds, at a value based on the tax appraisals made of their property by the owners themselves.

As the agrarian reform program caused a rift in the revolution inside Cuba and the first break in Cuban-American relations, it is worth examining closely. The right of a sovereign government to expropriate private property is a solidly established legal principle everywhere in the world. In Spanish law, moreover, fee simple land holdings do not exist, and all property is held on a contingent basis at the pleasure of the sovereign. Article 90 of the Cuban constitution of 1940 formally outlawed large estates, so that after that date *latifundios* continued to exist only because

the government failed to implement the law. The decree creating
the new National Institute of Agrarian Reform (INRA) was
therefore justifiable under both Cuban and international law.

The carrying out of the decree, however, was not in accord-
ance with the letter of the law. Officials of the INRA simply appeared on farms and took over everything in sight, including
buildings, trucks, livestock, and farm machinery. No inventories
were taken, and no receipts given. The farmland involved was
often worth as much as five or six times what it was listed for in
the assessment books, and Cuban 4.5 per cent bonds had fallen
to a third of their nominal value by mid-1960 (though Castro
continued to pay interest on them in dollars until the end of that
year). Furthermore, few of the bonds were actually printed, and
INRA officials were exasperatingly vague about their plans to
issue them. One American cattle ranch owner, whose importation
of purebred stock had made a definite contribution to the Cuban
agrarian economy, told me that he had waited nine months in
Havana without receiving a penny for his land or livestock. After
Congress and President Eisenhower eliminated the sugar quota
in July, 1960, Castro withdrew even his tenuous promise to pay
for American property unless Cuba were readmitted to the
American market.

One can, therefore, appreciate the grievances of such victims
of the agrarian reform, whom the Cubans call *siquitrillados*
("cicatrized ones"; literally, a fighting cock that has been mortally
wounded). Their plight, however, should not obscure the larger
picture, in which farms held by individuals were comparatively
unimportant. According to the Agricultural Census of 1946 more
than one-third of all the crop land in Cuba was owned by about
900 large corporations, some of them possessing as much as
610,000 acres. Small farmers working 25 acres or less had only
one-tenth as much land as was given over to the *latifundios*, and
this was generally the poorest land:

	Number	Holdings	Per cent of Farmland
Farms under 25 acres	62,500	730,000	3.3
Largest estates	894	8,000,000	36.

Between them the big sugar companies and the cattle ranchers owned 17 million acres and dominated Cuban agriculture. Sugar *latifundios* took up 22 per cent of the total land area of Oriente province, 27 per cent of Camaguey, and 36 per cent of Matanzas; the whole of the Isle of Pines, 3000 square kilometers, was owned by four landlords.

Under the American quota system and the International Sugar Agreement, production of Cuba's major crop was tightly controlled, with allowable sales rigidly parcelled out. The big companies could produce their quotas on about half their land; hence they let about three million acres lie fallow. Sugar is an intensely seasonal crop, requiring abundant labor only during the three- to four-month *zafra* (harvest) when the mills run twenty-four hours a day seven days a week. During these months, hundreds of thousands of cane cutters had to earn enough to enable them to survive until the next *zafra*. The system led to a cruel paradox: unemployment, poverty, and actual hunger in the presence of some of the most fertile (and unused) land in the world.

Although American investment in Cuba had been shifting away from agriculture since the 1930's, U.S.-owned companies still controlled 40 per cent of the sugar lands, including seven of the ten largest *latifundios*. The benefits of Cuban participation in the U.S. sugar quota, which have often been described as exemplifying generosity toward Cuba, actually worked primarily to the advantage of the big American companies. Most of the difference between the world price of sugar and the price paid by U.S. refineries went as profits to these dominant companies. The Cuban cane-cutters, who lived in poverty and hunger for most of the year, derived little benefit from the system.

In the early years of American occupation of the island, and under complaisant Cuban presidents thereafter, all kinds of *geofagia* ("earth-eating," the fraudulent seizure of land), tax evasion, and avoidance of labor legislation were possible. Cuban Atlantic, Cuban American, United Fruit and the rest had amortised their original investment decades ago, and put only a small part of their profits into new equipment and research (sugar yield per acre fell from 17.4 metric tons per acre before World War II to 15.5 in 1948). During the years 1935–1957 the eight largest American sugar firms made an average net profit of 23 per cent a year, most of which was sent to the United States in the form of interest and dividends. Well-to-do Cubans also built up nest eggs in American banks; despite the underdeveloped state of the Cuban economy, the island was actually exporting capital.

It is true that the assessed valuations upon which payment for expropriated land were to be based were unrealistically low. But the companies themselves set that valuation on their land; to complain of it is to accuse themselves of tax evasion under previous regimes. After visiting a few of these estates and seeing the poverty of men who have worked for twenty or thirty years for the United Fruit Company at Preston, for example, one becomes doubtful of the moral right of the corporation to payment in full, and in cash, for its property. As an INRA official said to me: "These people are in the position of a gambler who started out with ten cents and won a hundred dollars. They spent most of the hundred dollars, and we are giving them their ten cents back, but they want cash for all their chips." An American visitor might also compare the situation of the sugar companies to that of the Southern slaveholders, deprived by the Emancipation Proclamation and the Thirteenth Amendment of $4 billion worth of property, without even a promise to pay. Much injustice, confusion, and suffering resulted, but the end result was surely a forward step.

The year 1960, *"Año de la Reforma Agraria,"* was devoted to a massive reshaping of Cuban rural life. The INRA had begun with the properties that already belonged to the Cuban government, and with the extensive estates taken from Batista officials. Cattle lands were seized next, ostensibly to prevent their owners from slaughtering the herds and selling off the beef. The big sugar estates were taken after the 1960 harvest was complete; by the middle of the year the expropriation process was substantially complete, and not a single *latifundio* was left on the island.

It should be pointed out that the reform was directed against all large estates, Cuban as well as American, including the extensive holdings of the Castro family in Oriente.

In handling these properties that came under their control, the INRA's young men acted with understandable confusion, and, at least at first, with an amiable lack of ideology. The Soviet Union, for example, in its revolution stubbornly insisted on complete nationalization and the wiping out of all private landholdings; collectivization was accomplished only at an immense cost in suffering and in lives. The instigators of the Bolivian national revolution, on the other hand, were forced by circumstances to turn the land over to the Indians who were serfs on it, without being able to give them adequate credit or technical assistance; production has still not recovered its pre-reform levels. Mexico dragged out its agrarian reform for more than a generation, still has many large estates and landless farmers, and has not yet solved the problems of credit, marketing, and mechanization on many of its *ejidos* (communal farms).

Major Antonio Núñez Jiménez, the first director of INRA, and Carlos Rafael Rodríguez, the Communist professor and politician who succeeded him, have left about 40 per cent of Cuba's farmland, owned in parcels of less than one thousand acres, in the hands of its original owners. Another 20 per cent the land which was being worked by tenants, sharecroppers, or squatters, was turned over to them without charge, on the basis of a "vital minimum" of sixty-six acres per family of five. These farmers were individualists with a strong sense of private property, and were accustomed to working on their own. To have herded them into cooperatives would have conflicted with small holder habits. By cancelling their former burdensome rents and presenting them with handsomely engraved titles to the property they were cultivating, the revolution won for itself immediate popularity with this important social class.

These farmers, organized into the National Association of Small Farmers (ANAP), continue to play a key role in the Cuban economy. According to INRA's figures (which are admit-

tedly not precise but generally approximate the truth), after the
agrarian reform they owned 59 per cent of Cuba's arable land
and 76 per cent of her cattle. INRA, to be sure, retains control
of the lands that it has "turned over" to peasant proprietors. It
requires the owners to use INRA machinery and marketing facilities, and to plant the crops "suggested" by the local INRA office.
Couples who have been living together under the usual Cuban
common-law arrangement are not given land titles until they are
formally married. Proprietorship of such a severely circumscribed
kind would probably be considered "slavery" by Senator Goldwater or the American Farm Bureau, but it seems satisfactory to
most Cuban small holders. In Matanzas province, where over
one thousand titles to small farms were given out on July 26,
1960, all the new proprietors I talked with at the time were
pleased supporters of the new order. On a later visit, in 1962, I
found that some of their initial satisfaction at becoming landowners had worn off. Many of those I interviewed in Havana
and Las Villas provinces complained about shortages of fertilizer,
insecticides, and replacement parts for farm machinery, and the
near-total lack of new equipment. They felt that INRA gave
preferential treatment to the state-owned *granjas del pueblo*,
and that "we are making more money than before, sure, but
there's nothing to buy with your *pesos* now." But these complaints did not seem to me to be very much more serious than
those made by farmers everywhere in the world, even in the
United States. Counterrevolutionaries operating out of Miami
can expect little help from Cuba's small landholders.

On the rest of the land, which had been in big ranches or
sugar plantations, Fidel Castro himself made the decision (a
temporary one, as it proved) to move directly from the *latifundio*
to the collective farm, or cooperative. One of the first of these
to be established, the Cuba Libre cooperative in Matanzas, was
sixteen months old when I visited it in 1960, and may provide a
fair sample of the movement as a whole. The land, some 1400
acres, formerly belonged to a Batista official who fled to Miami
when the collapse came, so that no expropriation proceedings

were necessary. A lieutenant in the rebel army was sent in and the cooperative organized on March 10, 1959, the anniversary of Batista's second seizure of power. The *finca* (plantation) then had 800 acres planted in cane, and another 600 acres idle; the *guajiros* had not been allowed to have garden plots, or keep a cow, as that would have diminished the owner's profit from the company store.

Under the old system, when the last of the cane was cut and the rainy season began each May, the workers faced the dreaded eight months of *el tiempo muerto* ("the dead time"). During the "dead time" the men worked for as little as five dollars a month, and their income was less than $400 a year (the Cuban *peso* was at par with the dollar, and its purchasing power was about the same). When the harvest ended, the workers stopped eating meat, and used up the last kerosene in their lamps. After a few months there was no longer enough money left to buy even beans or rice, staple items in the Cuban diet. The *guajiros* turned to *malanga*, a potato-like root native to the island, or they went hungry. Under the Batista dictatorship, as under the ineffective "democracy" of Grau and Prío, there was no school, no doctor, no running water, no electricity, no toilet or even privy, no milk for the children (a can of condensed milk imported from the U.S. cost twenty-two cents in the owners' store). Only one in three or four of the adults was able to read or write even a little; education was of little value to a cane cutter to whom newspapers, magazines, and books were not available anyway.

With the founding of the cooperative, morale and living standards rose spectacularly. INRA's first step was to begin construction of concrete-block housing for the *cooperativistas*. These were modest but comfortable structures, with tile floors, electricity, running water, toilets, and roofs of processed *bagasse* (the crushed cane left after the sugar is extracted). Using mass production methods, and building without cellars or heating equipment (not needed in the Cuban climate), the INRA put these homes up for less than $2000 each. Title to them was given at once, with the cost to be paid out of the cooperatives' profits—but there have been no profits. In 1959 and 1960, before the economic squeeze and the diversion of materials and manpower to industry and defense, INRA's Department of Farm Homes built 30,000 such homes to replace the picturesque but squalid *bohío*. The newer model houses, with more rooms, better design, and concrete-slab roofs to offer better protection from the heat, are noticeably superior to those I saw at Cuba Libre. It will be many years—perhaps decades—before all of Cuba's farm workers are as well housed as this, but the homes already built are a positive sign of the regime's concern for the well-being of the long-neglected *guajiro,* and a promise of better things in the future.

Another innovation at Cuba Libre was the *tienda del pueblo,* or people's store, one of the more than 2000 operated by INRA. The old company store had operated on a markup of 100 per cent, often giving short weight and inferior goods and charging high interest. (Some of the workers still owed money on their parents' accounts, and one man showed me the record of a debt incurred by his grandfather that he had been paying off forty years later.) The new stores, which now get much of their merchandise from other cooperatives and state farms, charge only enough to break even on staple items, and make a small profit on toiletries, perfume, etc. In 1960 they were well-stocked, with items that farm people could not afford before—canned goods, shoes (especially important to prevent parasitic infections), toothpaste, light bulbs, and dozens of other items that most Americans never think about, but which were semi-luxuries in rural Cuba. By 1962, as a consequence of the cutting off of American trade, only rationed staples were available. But the farmers and fishermen I talked to took their privation in good part, and most of them still insisted that they were better off, morally and materially, than they had ever been before. During my stay at Cuba Libre a shipment of rice came in from the Antonio Maceo cooperative and a load of fish from a new co-op at Varadero Beach; this interchange of products is helpful in cost-cutting and in saving foreign exchange, for both rice and canned fish used to be imported from the United States. INRA also arranged to bring in a herd of fifty cows to supply milk at five cents a liter to the co-op and to the surrounding small farmers. The old disparity in living standards between Havana and Cuba's rural areas was being eliminated.

Another achievement of the agrarian reform is the provision of free medical and dental care, and the beginning of preventive medicine in an area that had known neither doctors nor hospitals. In 1959 Castro made a television appeal to younger doctors to serve voluntarily out in the countryside for six months, and many recent graduates of the newly-reopened medical school in Havana responded. I saw dozens of children in the Cuba Libre region brought in for polio shots; "under Batista," the young doctor at the clinic explained, "only the cattle were vaccinated." In 1962 infantile paralysis was all but eliminated in Cuba, following massive use of a Russian oral vaccine. The INRA dug wells to provide pure water, and built latrines for those who did not yet have new homes. A beginning was being made in checking parasitic diseases, which are a dreadful scourge all over Latin America, but the soil and water are so thoroughly polluted that it may take a generation to finish the job.

A final and most significant achievement of the cooperatives has been crop diversification and the use of formerly uncultivated land and unemployed laborers. To the 800 acres that were always in cane Cuba Libre's director added a number of new crops: 140 acres in potatoes, 70 in *judias* (black beans), 30 in peanuts, 40 in *fruta bomba* (melons), and 50 in forage crops for cattle. As the land had been fallow for many years, the crops did fairly well, despite the farmers' lack of experience in growing them. The INRA had also supplied eight new tractors and three pumps that were irrigating 700 acres.

My visit to Cuba Libre came during the middle of the "dead time." The seventy-one *cooperativistas* and their families, however, were busy harvesting potatoes and planting peanuts, clearing canefields and building new roads, so that there was an actual shortage of labor. People came in from the city of

Matanzas, and even from Havana on Sundays to help out with carpentry, road building, or in the fields. City workers who once looked down on the *guajiro* as a *bobo* (clown) have regularly volunteered to make a success of the revolution's agrarian program; much of the 1962 coffee crop and part of the 1963 sugar harvest were brought in by students and urban workers.

Despite serious difficulties that arose later, the agrarian reform won lasting support for the revolution in the Cuban countryside. The euphoria and utopian dreams of 1959 and 1960 wore away under the impact of the American blockade and the mismanagement and confusion that were inevitable in any program rushed through so rapidly and with so little preparation. But when I asked the Cuba Libre *cooperativistas* in 1960, the turkey raisers on a state farm in Pinar del Río in 1961, and the members of a fishermen's cooperative on the Bay of Pigs in 1962 whether they would like to do away with the Castro regime, the response was always an astonished stare, laughter, or an outburst of anger; and the fishermen had proved their loyalty with blood the previous year. Under Batista it had been a crime to own a firearm, or even a small penknife. But in 1960 the volunteer militia had an assortment of old pistols, nineteenth-century Krag-Jorgensens, and 1903 Springfields; in 1962, they had small Czechoslovak machine guns. The volunteers have no spit and polish about them, but they would make their island hard to conquer, as invaders discovered in 1961.

It was evident from the beginning that Castro was putting more money into the countryside than he could reasonably hope to get back for a long time to come. Cuba Libre, for example, received a $65,000 loan from INRA to finance its ambitious program of capital improvements, a sum it could not have paid back even had all the harvests gone according to plan (as they did not). The government, partly for political and partly for humanitarian reasons, decided to ignore both orthodox capitalist and Marxist procedures, and pump money into Cuba's rural economy. The results so far have been spotty and uneven. At the meeting of the First National Congress of Cane Cooperatives

in Havana in August, 1962, delegate after delegate explained to
me how badly things had been handled back on the farm. Ad-
ministrators, often PSP (Communist) politicians who knew more
about Marxism than manure, had failed to plan the work or to
supervise it properly; there was considerable shirking and absenteeism, and some sabotage. Unfamiliar crops like corn, rice,
and tomatoes were planted in unsuitable soil, not fertilized, and
not cultivated; often the entire crop was lost. On some cooperatives the men were not paid for months at a time, and had to dig
up and eat immature crops or go to work for nearby private
owners. Sugar production, hurt by mismanagement and a dry
spell, slumped badly, from 6.6 million tons in 1961 to 4.8 million
tons in 1962, an output that had been exceeded as far back as
1925. Guevara, never given to mincing words, confessed that

We had an agricultural production that was much lower because
there were defects in organization, subjectivism in the planning of
production, and, furthermore, an extraordinary drought. I put the
drought last because I don't wish to excuse our errors with that as an
explanation. I merely add it as a partial explanation of the relative
drop in agriculture.

The practical knowledge of the farm workers, which the
regime had relied on to replace the old *capataz* (foreman) proved
illusory; as a Bulgarian agronomist complained to me, "these
people know only how to plant cane, cut cane, march in parades,
dance the cha-cha-cha, and nothing else." Some cooperativists
and private farmers had also taken to selling their produce on
the black market, to people who drove out into the countryside
in automobiles or buses, instead of delivering it to INRA at low
fixed prices. As an interesting insight into the regime's class bias,
the farmers involved were generally going unpunished (at least
in mid-1962), while middle-class people caught with more than
twenty-five pounds of food in their cars have been jailed for as
long as six months. Production of staple items like beans, rice,

and corn did increase,* but not as much as had been planned, and not enough to take the place of what had formerly been imported from the United States. In 1963, after turning the cooperatives into state farms, Carlos Rafael Rodríguez complained that a disappointing rice harvest was caused by "the bad faith of the workers in the fields and the absence of fraternity in many agricultural units due to a lack of adequate political work."

The result of these difficulties and mistaken and similar ones in the factories, added to the loss of over $500 million in imports from the United States, has been a shortage of just about every consumer good. As Castro himself admitted, "We are ashamed. Who is to blame? The administrators, the rulers, everyone." The food ration makes a sorry showing to Americans accustomed to the splendor of their local supermarket: 6 pounds of rice, 1½ pounds of beans, 1 pound of lard, and 1 cake of soap a month; 1 egg and ¾ pound of meat a week; less than 1 glass of milk a day (except for children under seven). Clothing and shoes, in short supply and shabby in quality for many months, were put on the ration list in February, 1963, and Castro's promises of plenty have been postponed to an indefinite future.

It would be dangerous to delude ourselves into thinking that these problems, serious as they are, are going to bring about the collapse of the regime; Herbert Hoover made that mistake in the 1920's when he declared that the Soviet Union could never "return to production." The Cuban diet at the beginning of 1963 was

Cuban Agricultural Production
(in thousands of metric tons)

	1958	1961
Beans	33	59
Rice	163	213
Corn	134	198
Cotton	0	14

[INRA figures, quoted in *Hispanic American Report* (Stanford), January, 1963, 1009.] Cuban agricultural statistics as a rule have a touch of poetry about them; but since these come from the same report in which a severe drop in sugar production is admitted they seem likely to be reasonably accurate.

scanty and monotonous, but sufficient; many *guajiros* are eating
better than under previous governments because they have regular work, and what food is available is shared equally. Certainly
the food situation was not nearly as bad as it was in the U.S.S.R.
in the 1930's, nor as it is reported to be in China today; and it
is far above the semi-starvation level that has prevailed in Bolivia,
Guatemala, Haiti, Paraguay, Highland Peru, rural Mexico, and
northeast Brazil for decades.

With salaries frozen and consumer goods unavailable, the
Cubans tried to replace the old capitalist incentives to work
with such new ones as patriotism, altruism, a sense of sacrifice,
and what they call "Socialist emulation." Even the regime's bit-
terest enemies have grudgingly paid tribute to the personal (if
not political) honesty and devotion to duty of the tight little
group of young *barbudos* and old Communists who run the revolution. There is no sign, so far, of the kind of corruption at the
top described by Milovan Djilas in *The New Class;* as the Minister of Basic Industries, Señor Saenz, said to me with a grin, "The
only privilege I have is the right to work harder than anybody
else." One of the two or three dozen most powerful figures in the
government, he lived in a modest housing development, with
a schoolteacher next door on one side and a rebel army lieutenant
on the other; he didn't even have a telephone at home, although
he desperately needed one. He drove to work in a battered old
Buick, which he had purchased under the previous regime and
never replaced; when I interviewed him he had been working
eighty to ninety hours a week without a vacation for more than
two years.

Many Cubans, especially educated and middle-class people,
do not respond to these new incentives, and are naturally hostile
to a regime that has brought about a catastrophic drop in their
standard of living. These are the people—lawyers, businessmen,
doctors, teachers, engineers, skilled workers—who have fled Cuba
by the tens of thousands, who feel that the regime they helped
bring to power has betrayed them, who engaged in sabotage inside Cuba and made up the bulk of the 1500-man force that
invaded the island in 1961. Castro, unwilling to slow down the

headlong pace of the revolution and unable to brook opposition to his plans (whatever they might be at any given moment), turned all the apparatus of a police state against what he calls these *gusanos* (worms). The twenty-year jail sentence meted out to Major Hubert Matos late in 1959 because he attacked growing Communist influence and tried to sponsor mass resignations from the army was an early sign of Castro's ruthlessness. The suppression of independent newspapers, the muzzling of radio and television, the conversion of Cuba's labor unions into organs of an all-powerful state, and the organization of the Soviet-style United Party of the Socialist Revolution (PURS) followed in due course. On May 1, 1961, Castro formally stated (what was already obvious) that his was a "Socialist" revolution; in December he declared that he "believe[d] absolutely in Marxism [and would] be a Marxist-Leninist until the last day of [his] life."

Cuba's drive toward totalitarianism was accompanied by (and at least in part caused by) a rapid worsening of Cuban-American relations. Castro seems from the beginning to have operated without any fixed ideological base, making policy as he went along. He came into power suspicious of American intentions toward him, and he reacted violently—too violently—to every real or imaginary injury coming from the North. The Eisenhower and Kennedy administrations (whose Cuban policies were indistinguishable, except for changes in rhetoric and personnel) replied with countermeasures which were not sufficient to overthrow Castro and succeeded only in making him more violent and reckless than ever.

Castro was certainly not "driven into" the arms of Khrushchev in the sense that he had no choice at all in the matter. Time and again, in reviewing the endless speeches and violent turmoil of his first four years in power, one is struck by his refusal to compromise, to yield to the dictates of prudence, to allow for geographic, economic, and political realities. One looks in vain for common sense and moderation in a man who would never have become a revolutionary or overthrown Batista if he had possessed very much of either. Castro was evidently not a Communist when he came to power or for a long time afterwards. On this question the testimony of Deputy CIA Director, General C. P. Cabell, before the Senate Internal Security Committee on November 5, 1959, was clear: "We believe that Castro is not a member of the Communist Party, and does not consider himself to be a Communist."

But, given Castro's impetuous personality and the willingness of domestic and Soviet Communists to go along with and encourage his anti-*Yanqui* sentiments, he could easily be made into their ally. American diplomacy, by its initial failure to reach some sort of understanding with Castro in the early part of 1959, and by its implacable hostility to his regime afterwards, simply abandoned the field to Khrushchev, Mikoyan, and their Cuban counterparts. When the United States abolished the Cuban sugar quota and placed an embargo on shipments of crude oil to the island, the U.S.S.R. was ready and more than willing to move into the gap.

More skillful American diplomacy might have caused events to move in a very different direction, especially in the early months of 1959, when Castro's thinking had not yet hardened into a pro-Soviet mold. It is easy to forget, now, that Fidel's first cabinet was made up of moderates and even conservatives; that his first visit abroad was to the United States; that in 1959 he sponsored a multi-million-dollar publicity campaign to attract American tourists; that he promised to pay (in bonds) for the lands taken by the Agrarian Reform Law; that he continued to pay interest in dollars on Cuban bonds traded on the New York Stock Exchange for two years after coming to power; that he still insists that he is willing to reimburse American owners of expropriated property if Cuba is allowed to earn dollars by selling sugar to the United States. The good old days of big American profits from sugar, gambling, oil refining, and the telephone and electricity monopolies were over the day the *barbudos* rode into Havana. And dealing with a proud, impulsive, complicated man like Castro is not easy; but surely a flexible, realistic policy could have done much to save the situation.

Instead, there was a series of falsifications and blunders by Eisenhower and Kennedy, Congress and the State Department,

the wire services and public opinion which they had helped to
misinform. Eisenhower's Cuban policy was marked by hypocritical clamor over the trials of Batista's thugs (nobody had complained about the fate of their victims); by the summoning of
Batista officials to testify before a Senate committee; by cane-
burning raids of light planes operating out of Florida; by repeated
warnings that they must pay for expropriated American property
at once, and in cash; by abolition of the sugar quota; by bribing
of defectors and supplying of saboteurs; by the recruiting and
training of a band of Cuban exiles in Florida and Guatemala; and,
finally, by the breaking of diplomatic relations and the imposition
of a travel ban a few weeks before Kennedy's inauguration.

Castro replied to these pressures as anyone who knew him
could have predicted—with defiance and vigorous countermeasures. He *had* to take stern measures against dissent and
sabotage or go down under American pressure as Grau did in
1933 or Arbenz did in 1955. No one but an apologist for Fidel
would completely condone the mass arrests and police state
measures at the time of the 1961 invasion, but we must try to
understand them. What would the state of civil liberties be in
Florida if Soviet-supplied guerrillas were operating in the swamps,
hundreds of orange groves set afire, the largest department store
in Miami burned to the ground, the oil depots and power plant
bombed, and fifteen hundred Negro "freedom fighters" landed on
the coast from a Russian flotilla? Castro turned to the Russians
because they were willing and able to keep his revolution afloat
in the face of American hostility; and he turned to the local Communists, as one of them explained it to me, "because he's sure *we*
aren't going to run off to Miami the day after tomorrow." Thus
our military aid to Batista and our pressures on Castro helped
bring about what we most feared, the intrusion of Soviet Communism in the Caribbean.

I visited Cuba for the second time in the waning days of the
Eisenhower administration, and I remember the cautious optimism that one Foreign Office subordinate expressed about the
incoming Democratic President. He thought Kennedy's television
belligerence might be "just politics," and hoped the new President

would be as willing to negotiate with Castro as with Khrushchev. Eighteen months later that official admitted he was wrong. The change of administrations provided a natural opportunity for a new look at our Cuban policy, which had certainly been disastrous up to that time. But so far as the public record shows, Kennedy never made the slightest effort to come to some sort of agreement with the revolutionary regime to the south. Instead he reappointed Allen Dulles and told him to keep on training his Cuban invasion army; he continued the travel ban and the suspension of diplomatic relations and proclaimed a complete embargo on shipments to Cuba; he tried to appoint a crony, Earl E. T. Smith, formerly Ambassador to Cuba, as Ambassador to Switzerland—the nation which presently handles our relations with Cuba; he launched the disastrous landing at Playa Girón; he successfully pressured a majority of the other Latin states (but not the largest ones) into breaking relations with Castro; he had Cuba thrown out of the OAS; he cut off Castro's last trickle of dollars by barring the import of Cuban fruit and cigars; he sponsored a world-wide economic blockade of the island; and he did not prevent continued sabotage and naval raids by Cuban exiles operating out of Miami and Puerto Rico.

Mutual suspicion and fear between the United States and her diminutive neighbor came to a climax in October, 1962. Castro permitted (or, more likely, encouraged) the emplacement of Russian missiles on Cuban soil, perhaps as a political-military gesture of defiance, perhaps to deter a possible American invasion; Kennedy had to go to the edge of war to get them out. As Khrushchev noted in one of his letters to the President, events seemed to be getting out of hand; a miscalculation, an accident, a bit of misplaced truculence could have swept the world into the inferno of nuclear war. Had war come, the holocaust would have been so great as to make the issue of war guilt meaningless; Khrushchev's reckless invasion of the Caribbean with bombers and missiles, Castro's willingness to wrap the Caribbean (and perhaps the world) in flames rather than yield to American pressures, and Kennedy's adoption of the Dulles strategy of "brinkmanship" and "massive retaliation" could have been given about equal blame for bringing on the catastrophe.

As events proved, the President was right about the Russian reaction to his challenge—this time. He won a stunning diplomatic victory. One must be grateful for the President's refusal to yield to the War Hawks who recommended an immediate invasion of Cuba, and for his iron control over the reconnaissance planes and naval units in the Caribbean. But the long-range results of the confrontation of wills remain to be seen. We cannot afford to win many more victories of this kind. It took the threat of nuclear war to obtain the limited objectives of getting missiles and bombers out of Cuba; surely there was an alternative policy which, pursued earlier, would have avoided their being sent to the island in the first place. Our implacable hostility to Castro has not yielded any results except to embitter him, lower the living standard of the Cuban people, and make a more independent course on Cuba's part impossible even if her leader wanted to pursue it. Yet, as the Cuban revolution enters its fifth year, we are apparently convinced that we have no alternative except to destroy it; the last word is still Adlai Stevenson's remark at the United Nations during the missile crisis that "the maintenance of a Communist regime in the Western Hemisphere is not negotiable."

Trying to predict the future course of the Cuban revolution is an imposing task, depending as it does on decisions to be made in Washington, Moscow, and Peking, as well as in Havana. It is not even easy to know what is happening inside Cuba today; Cuban propaganda and American counterpropaganda are available, but impartial comment by neutral observers is hard to find. My own visits to the island, brief and far between as they were, left me with the definite feeling that the regime would last; in spite of shortages, rationing, the menace of invasion, and the contrary evidence of the refugee exodus, Castro still seemed to have the backing of a substantial majority of the Cuban people. Other recent and uncommitted observers have had the same impression.

As long as the United States continues to exert massive

pressures against the regime, of course, it will remain insecure. Khrushchev may eventually decide that his uneasy alliance with Castro, which has tied up half his tanker fleet, cost him about $1 million a day, and exposed him to a humiliating defeat in 1962, is too expensive to be worth while. But this is hardly likely. The whole Communist *mystique* is heavily dependent on the promise of an inevitable and world-wide victory; the Soviet Union is too deeply committed in Cuba to pull back now. Moreover, the expense of supporting the revolution is small enough compared to what the United States spends on its similar outposts in South Korea, Formosa, and South Vietnam.

If the present uncomfortable truce between Castro and Kennedy continues, and we make no direct move to overthrow his government, Cuba's long-range economic prospects are not at all bad. Ideology aside, the island's resources are so great in relation to its population that any reasonably sensible productive system will make the Cubans more prosperous than they have ever been under American tutelage. Cuba's soil is fertile and plentiful, and as the Cubans say, *"Esta tierra nunca duerme"* ("This land never sleeps"); i.e., there is no frost and you can grow two and in places three crops a year if there is irrigation in the dry season. Cuba presently produces commercial quantities of manganese, chrome, nickel, and copper, and has enormous unexploited reserves of iron ore; a recent Soviet geological survey indicates that there may be oil, and half a dozen wells are being drilled. While hardship and sacrifice are still ahead, Cuba's ordeal should be vastly easier than those of Britain during the London blitz, Russia facing German attack, or China today—and none of those countries cracked under pressure.

If Castro's government-by-direct-rapport survives, what will it be like? Theodore Draper, who has studied Fidel's public pronouncements as carefully as anyone, has issued a sobering warning:

At bottom, all these "neo" and "direct" democracies rest on a simple proposition: that the leader and his people are one and indivisible. Hence they need no representative institutions, no elections, no loyal or disloyal oppositions, no free or partially critical press, none of the rights and safeguards traditionally associated with a democracy.

The horror of this thinking is that it wipes out the lessons to be learned from the most desperate and tragic experiences of our time. If there is anything that should have burned itself into our consciousness, it is the excruciating evil of the popular despot, the beloved dictator, the mass leader. [*Castro's Revolution.*]

There is certainly a disturbing similarity between the attitude of the young girl from the "Carlos Marx" Secondary School whom I once watched pin a medal on Fidel and the adoring *Mädchen* so often seen in propaganda shots of Adolf Hitler. There is no *institutional* guarantee against Fidel's turning into a Caribbean version of *Der Fuehrer.* All the rapidly developing new organizations of the revolution—the INRA, the Union of Secondary School Students, the Union of Young Communists, the labor unions, the army, and the militia—are subject to his control and shaped by his will. Fidel can, with a single televised speech, destroy a conservative president (Manuel Urrutia Lleo, July, 1959) or an overambitious Communist bureaucrat (Aníbal Escalante, March, 1962). He has had people shot for burning cane fields (the same kind of sabotage he used against the dictatorship that preceded his own), and grown increasingly harsh with workers who "do not understand what socialism is." He can organize cooperatives in 1959, change them into state farms in 1962, give out land titles today and take them back tomorrow: no one can set limits to his power inside Cuba, or say just what he will do with it.

But in defense of Fidel it must be said at once that he is no Hitler, no Stalin. His particular brand of Marxism is purposeful and tough-minded, but not brutal. His enemies have lost their property, but not—unless they committed atrocities before 1959, or took up arms against the revolution afterward—their lives. Middle- and upper-class Cubans, unlike the French aristocracy in 1792, Russian kulaks in the 1930's, and Chinese landlords in the 1950's, have been allowed to choose between joining the new regime or going into exile—a hard choice, but vastly preferable to death in a concentration camp. Judged by the number of executions (less than 2000, mostly of men convicted of murder or captured with arms in their hands) or the number of exiles (about 200,000), this is the mildest revolution since our own, back in 1775. I would not excuse police state measures of any kind, but there are degrees of repression. One way to measure the distance between Castro's Cuba and a completely tyrannical regime such as Ulbricht's East Germany is to compare the two planeloads of refugees that were permitted to leave for Miami every day before Pan American cancelled the flights with the murderous watch kept along the Berlin Wall; another is to contrast the Cuban people, encouraged and even pressured into bearing arms in the militia, with the cowed and defenseless workers of East Germany. Cuba today is certainly not the deliriously happy island of January 1959, or the workers' paradise described by C. Wright Mills and Jean-Paul Sartre; but it is not Stalin's Russia, either. The elimination of racial barriers, the literacy campaign (for all its doctrinaire Marxist teaching), the new educational opportunities for lower class children, the housing program, the workers' vacation resorts, the wiping out of graft and prostitution, the schools and hospitals I have seen on my three visits to the island must be taken into account in making any fair appraisal of the Castro regime.

When I first visited Cuba, in 1960, I thought (perhaps mistakenly) that it was still possible to win Castro to some sort of neutrality, that we might persuade him to follow a non-Communist leftist-nationalist line similar to that of Guinea's Sékou Touré or Egypt's Nasser. If there was any such possibility in 1960, it seems exceedingly remote in 1963, destroyed by America's unwavering hostility, Castro's intransigence, or both. If President Kennedy keeps his tacit 1962 promise not to invade Cuba, and if the noisy Cuban refugees in Miami are as powerless as I think they are, we are going to have to get along with a Communist neighbor only 90 miles from Florida—though it is hard to imagine an American Congressman, Senator, or President quite daring to admit this.

But there are Communists and Communists, and circumstances alter cases. We were allied, once, with even so brutal a dictator as Joseph Stalin; it is possible to imagine that we may eventually find ourselves reaching some sort of arrangement with one of his successors, perhaps in opposition to China's relentless belligerence. In that event, United States–Soviet Union–Cuban relations would be seen in a new aspect, as they were during the missile crisis, when Khrushchev and Kennedy temporarily found themselves in agreement (and in opposition to Castro). We have also the examples of Poland and Yugoslavia as guideposts to the degree to which Communist regimes may be softened and led to permit a certain amount of civil liberty; Gomulka and Tito are no more tyrannical than any one of a dozen dictators in what we like to call the "free world." It seems senseless for us to try to increase diplomatic, commercial, and cultural relations in Warsaw, Belgrade, and Moscow, while resolutely refusing to have anything to do with a regime geographically so much closer to us, in Havana.

We may have to learn, then, to live with Castro, just as Britain has learned to live with Nasser, and Khrushchev has had to patch up Stalin's quarrel with Tito. President Kennedy, at any rate, seemed to recognize this unpleasant fact when he rejected advice that he send troops into Cuba in 1961 and 1962; CIA director John A. McCone has testified that nothing less than this will serve to bring Castro down. And Castro, for all his truculence, will have to learn to live with the United States. Ideology and emotion may have shaped his policy so far, but geography and economic realities must prove decisive in the long run; it makes no sense to ship Cuban sugar to China or Russia or to depend on the U.S.S.R. for 80 per cent of Cuba's imports. As Brazil's Kubitschek remarked, in a phrase that is doubtless as wounding to Castro's sensibilities as our own, "It is time for both Cuba and the United States to act the part of grown men." We have certainly not been playing a sensible role in our quarrel with a nation whose annual income of $2.8 billion is about equal to what we spend on cosmetics each year.

Our disastrous Cuban experience will have been of some use

if it teaches us something about how to deal with the social revolutions that are surely coming elsewhere to the south. Cuba, for all its strategic location, is an underdeveloped island of only seven million people whose principal product is utterly nonstrategic. Castro himself is a nuisance and an annoyance, a gnat stinging the American elephant. But, deprived of Russian rockets, he cannot menace American security directly. Fidelismo will really threaten us only if this kind of Communist revolution spreads to major Latin nations such as Argentina, Brazil, Chile, and Venezuela. If we are to keep this from happening, we need to think through again the unhappy record of our Cuban diplomacy during the past few years and decades. And for a lesson in how we might better have dealt with the Cuban Revolution, we can profit from the study of our relations with Mexico, which went through a similar social upheaval beginning more than half a century ago.

CHAPTER 7

Mexico: After the Revolution

This country is a laboratory for trying out new, and what we would call radical, policies. If Mexico can have quiet and progressive policies in the interests of Mexicans and not of foreigners, it may solve some problems here which may benefit other nations less able to try experiments.
                    Josephus Daniels (1934)
                    quoted in E. David Cronon,
                    Josephus Daniels in Mexico (1960)
We are realistic revolutionaries, not utopian dreamers.
                    President Adolfo López Mateos (1961)

Political evolution, like its biological counterpart, does not proceed at an even, predictable pace. The social structure of nations such as Peru may remain unchanged for centuries, while that of Uruguay is gradually developing toward democracy and social justice; nations as different as Bolivia and Cuba may be caught up in revolutionary crises within the same decade. In some parts of Latin America the forces for change seem non-existent; a medieval curiosity such as General Alfredo Stroessner's Paraguay is as unlikely in the middle of the twentieth century as the horseshoe crab which so troubled Henry Adams because it "appeared to be identical from the beginning to the end of geological time." And sometimes nations appear to be evolving backwards, from modern democracy to military rule, as Argentina did in the 1930's and Cuba did after the civil regimes of Grau San Martín and Prío Socarrás a decade later.

If the details of change are uncertain, the broad outlines of development are clear. The caudilloships *are* outmoded, and will

105

persist, if at all, only in marginal, out-of-the-way nations. All the "westernizing" forces at loose in the modern world—technology, nationalism, growing literacy, urbanization, increased trade in goods and ideas—inevitably call for some form of mass participation in the political process. Analogies are apt to mislead through oversimplification; but as a horse is a higher form of life than a snail, it is similarly clear that nations like Chile or Colombia are more advanced than Nicaragua or Haiti. Some changes, moreover, are permanent. Once a real social revolution has taken place it is impossible to restore the old order. Looked at from the evolutionary point of view, the most advanced forms of Latin American government, the political equivalent of *homo sapiens*, are Uruguay and Mexico, the only nations that have passed through genuine revolutions and proved it by decades of political stability. Mexico's history over the past half century provides us with an excellent opportunity to consider the process of revolutionary change, the relations of revolutionary governments with the United States, and the kind of post-revolutionary regimes other Latin American countries may well develop in the future.

Modern Mexican history begins with the thirty-five year reign of the greatest of all the *caudillos*, Porfirio Díaz, a shrewd Mixtec Indian who dominated the national life in 1876 to 1911. Taking over the country racked by decades of civil war, religious strife, and foreign intervention, Díaz ruthlessly suppressed his rivals, balanced the budget, and "made Mexico one of the safest countries in the world—except for Mexicans." During the latter part of his rule, the dictator surrounded himself with the *científicos*, an able, if narrow-minded group of Social Darwinists who despised Mexico's Indian masses and worshipped economic development. Under their rule, Mexico experienced tranquillity and progress—of a sort. The statistics of the Porfirian peace as reported by John A. Crow in *Mexico Today*, were impressive:

	1876	1911
Railroad lines	700 km.	25,000 km.
Foreign trade	50 million *pesos*	500 million *pesos*
Federal income	20 million *pesos*	110 million *pesos*
U. S. investment	$50 million	$1 billion

With foreign capital flowing in, gold and silver production rose 400 percent, Mexico became the world's second largest producer of copper, and the oil industry shot up from almost nothing to 13 million barrels in 1911.

But these notable economic advances brought no benefits whatever to those outside the charmed circle of the Army, the Church, the favored politicians, the foreign investors, and the few thousand *hacendados* who gathered into their hands during these years whatever lands were left to the Indian communities. Professor Frank Tannenbaum gives some striking examples of the degree to which land ownership was concentrated:

Three haciendas occupied the 186 miles between Saltillo and Zacatecas. The properties of the Terrazas family in Chihuahua were comparable in extent to Costa Rica. In the state of Hidalgo the Central Railroad passed through the Escandon estates for a distance of about 90 miles. In Lower California foreign companies owned 78 per cent of the land, an area greater than Ireland. The haciendas of La Honda and Santa Catalina in Zacatecas contained about 419,000 acres. The state of Morelos belonged to thirty-two families, and the census of 1910 recorded only 834 *hacendados* in all Mexico. [*Mexico: The Struggle for Peace and Bread.*]

When individuals or tribes like the Yaquis of Sonora fought to retain their lands, they were crushed by federal troops and sold as laborers, at so much a head, to the plantations in Quintana Roo. Behind the facade of the handsomely rebuilt capital was a land of misery and terror.

As Díaz grew older (he was elected for the last time at eighty), his control of the nation weakened, and Mexico's unresolved social tensions grew worse. Shortly after the elaborate celebration of the centenary of Mexico's independence in 1910, Francisco Madero, a mild-mannered landlord's son, raised the standard of revolt from across the border, in San Antonio, Texas. His initial invasion attempt was easily suppressed, but unexpected allies soon rose all over the country; Pancho Villa, a peon turned bandit in Chihuahua, Venustiano Carranza, a *hacendado* and governor of Coahuila, the illiterate sharecropper Emiliano Zapata in Morelos, and small guerrilla bands in every state from Sonora and Baja California down to tropical Yucatán. The seemingly invincible dictatorship crumbled; in May, 1911, Díaz resigned and went into exile.

The history of the next decade is one of intermittent bloodshed and civil war. Madero briefly came to the presidency, to be betrayed and murdered by Victoriano Huerta, one of Díaz' generals, who drunkenly tried to restore the *porfirista* regime. Then Huerta was overthrown by a shaky coalition whose leaders immediately began fighting among themselves; Carranza eventually made good his title of First Chief, and called a convention which wrote a new (and revolutionary) constitution in 1917. Trying to keep power too long, Carranza was deposed and shot in 1920; under Álvaro Obregón, an able and realistic rancher from the North, Mexico at last entered the peaceful phase of her revolution.

Obregón (1920–1924), and his successor Plutarco Elías Calles (1924–1928), continued to rule with strong-arm methods reminiscent of Don Porfirio. Graft, rigged elections, and the occasional murder of political opponents continued to represent the truth behind the revolutionary slogans. But progress and social reform had become a permanent part of Mexican life, and neither Presidents nor local bosses could ignore continuing demands for more of both. A rural school program sent hundreds of dedicated young people out to the villages to teach the alphabet, arithmetic, sanitation, and the rudiments of scientific agriculture. The labor movement, though rent by factionalism and bribery, grew powerful and brought about a gradual improvement in wages and working conditions. And the agrarian reform, the touchstone of the revolution in a nation still overwhelmingly rural, continued to move forward, although with disappointing slowness and corruption. Obregón distributed some three million acres, Calles eight million during the four years of his official presidency, most of it to communal villages, or *ejidos*.

Under the three puppet presidents who followed Calles, and whom he controlled, the Revolution slowed down and seemed to have come to a stop. The labor unions were broken by the same government tactics that had built them up, and wages fell as the force of the world-wide depression struck the still feeble Mexican economy. Calles and his cronies, now grown enormously wealthy, declared that the agrarian program was a mistake, that the *ejido* did not produce efficiently; the amount of land distributed fell from two and a half million acres in 1929 to half a million in 1933. Except for its revived (and this time pointless) campaign against the Catholic Church, the government seemed to have completely abandoned its commitment to the goals of the Revolution.

But enough of Mexico's people had become politically active to make any further drift toward reaction dangerous. Bowing to demands from the younger politicians, Calles picked for his fourth President, Lázaro Cárdenas, a thirty-nine-year-old dark horse with a reputation for honesty and devotion to reform in his native state of Michoacán. Calles chose his Cabinet and expected to control his administration, but Cárdenas really intended to fulfill the promises of the Revolution, and when Calles got in the way he was exiled to California. This was the first of many useful precedents; previous deposed leaders such as Madero, Zapata, Carranza, Villa, and Obregón had been assassinated or "shot while attempting to escape."

During his six years in office Cárdenas pushed through reform measures far more drastic than anything being tried by the New Dealers on the other side of the Rio Grande. The labor unions were reorganized, this time on a permanent basis, and made part of the renamed official Party of the Mexican Revolution (PRM). When Cárdenas came into office all his predecessors together had distributed only twenty million acres of land; in six years he gave out considerably more than twice as much, benefiting three-quarters of a million peasant families. When the foreign oil companies refused to comply with a court-approved wage increase, Cárdenas unhesitatingly nationalized them, and managed to ride out the subsequent boycott and diplomatic pressure.

Above all Cárdenas restored the *mystique* of the Revolution by his personal example. Inflexibly honest (though some of his relatives and officials indulged in graft), he spent most of his term travelling through Mexico's thousands of villages, listening to needs and complaints and trying to answer them from his government's still meager resources. An anecdote reported by Anita Brenner in *The Wind That Swept Mexico* indicates his approach to Mexico's problems:

The current joke was that one morning while dispatching business in the capital his secretary laid a list of urgent matters, and a telegram, before him. The list said: *Bank reserves dangerously low.* "Tell the Treasurer," said Cárdenas. *Agricultural production falling.* "Tell the Minister of Communications." *Serious message from Washington.* "Tell Foreign Affairs." Then he opened the telegram, which read: "My corn dried, my burro died, my sow was stolen, my baby is sick. Signed, Pedro Juan, village of Huitzlipituzco."

"Order the presidential train at once," said Cárdenas. "I am leaving for Huitzlipituzco."

Cárdenas' insistence on personally handling even minor governmental details reminds one of Fidel Castro's endless tours of the Cuban countryside, and was doubtless as inefficient from an administrative point of view. But in Latin nations without organized party or governmental structures, where personalities count for so much, an energetic and perhaps dictatorial reformist chief may be the only one who can get things done.

Cárdenas' final and perhaps most important contribution to Mexico's welfare was his decision to leave office quietly, and to retire temporarily from politics. In this way he permitted his successor, the rather colorless Manuel Ávila Camacho, to come into power without the struggle that had attended the inauguration of every President since 1910. The precedent thus set has been followed. The businessman Miguel Alemán in 1946, the honest bureaucrat Ruiz Cortines in 1952, and the middle-of-the-road reformer Adolfo López Mateos in 1958 have all taken office as peacefully as their American contemporaries Truman, Eisenhower, and Kennedy, and their record in office (considering the vastly different problems and resources of Mexico and the United States) has been at least as good.

What kind of a government has evolved out of Mexico's fifty years of revolution, first bloody and now "institutional"? The key to the system is the dominant Party of Revolutionary Institutions (PRI), which, like the Democrats in Georgia or Alabama, never loses an election. The party automatically wins the presidency and currently controls all the Governors, all the Senators, and 172 of the 178 Federal deputies. At first only another ephemeral tool of Calles, the PRI has grown so strong that it is now, like the major American parties, far more important than any individual. Even Cárdenas' continuing personal popularity counts for little against the massive weight of the party machinery; he has been unable, for example, to attract much of a following in his recent pro-Castro campaign.

Americans, accustomed to two-party systems in the English-speaking countries and to multi-party contests in Western Europe, may look askance at a one-party government and refuse to believe that it can be democratic. It is true that opposition parties and candidates stand little chance of winning office, and that the government sometimes abuses its power. The eight-year prison sentence meted out to the famous painter (and Communist) David Alfaro Siqueiros under the vague Law of Social Dissolution, and the unpunished murder of peasant leader Rubén Jaramillo by Army units in 1962 are survivals of strong-arm methods from the days of Don Porfirio. (Lest we grow too complacent about our own political virtues, let us remember similar treatment of Communists, Southern Negroes, and dissident members of the teamsters' or longshoremen's unions in our own country.)

But the PRI is, in its own way, responsive to public opinion and to the demands of Mexico's masses. Some components of the governmental machine, it is true, get an unduly large part of the nation's resources. Robert E. Scott reports in *Mexican Government in Transition* that

Between 1952 and 1958 . . . Mexico's 300,000 government bureaucrats were granted special benefits in the form of raises, cost-of-living grants, and year-end bonuses equivalent to a month's salary, to the total of over 900 million pesos. This is the equivalent of 75 million dollars . . . and just over three percent of the total national budget expenditures for the period. . . .

During the period 1939–1950, real income rose for the fourteen percent of Mexicans not in the lower class who obtained their income from capital, salaries, etc., while it fell for the eighty-six percent in the lower class who earned their living from rural and urban labor and services. . . . A government agency, reported that in 1955 one percent of the gainfully employed got fifty-six percent of the national cash income and ninety-nine percent the remaining forty-four percent.

But the ruling elite in any country, the United States and the Soviet Union not excluded, always get more than their share of the national wealth. The PRI, unlike one-party Communist regimes, does permit opposition newspapers and parties to function, and there is a considerable and growing amount of democracy within the party, with the component elements of labor, farm groups, and the so-called "Popular Sector" struggling for influence and economic favors. We must measure the PRI's accomplishments not against some imaginary, utopian political system, but against real governments existing elsewhere in the underdeveloped world, and by that yardstick Mexico's regime comes off very well indeed. Under the PRI, Mexico has enjoyed more liberty and stability than any other Latin government. It is illuminating, for example, to compare the date of Mexico's present constitution (1917) with those of her Central American neighbors: Costa Rica (1949); El Salvador (1950); Nicaragua (1950); Honduras (1936; suspended 1954); Guatemala (1956; suspended 1963).

One consequence of this stability has been an impressive record of economic growth. Between 1940 and 1957 the Gross National Product increased at an average rate of 6 percent a year, and per capita income increased from $60 to $270. In the twelve years after 1945 the growth of heavy industry was particularly spectacular; the production of crude oil and electricity doubled, oil refining and cement output tripled, and the production of steel increased 500 percent. More remarkable still, in view of the fact that only 10 percent of the country (about 50 million acres) is arable, agricultural production also doubled during the same years. Mechanization, the increased use of fertilizers and improved seed varieties, and especially a massive irrigation program have pushed Malthusian fears of starvation off into the future.

The economic boom has slowed down somewhat in recent years, but production increases still manage to stay ahead of the rise in population; the national growth rate was 4.6 percent in 1958, 4.7 percent in 1959, 5.7 percent in 1960, 3.5 percent in 1961, and about 5 percent (estimated) in 1962. The Mexican economy, though still vulnerable to commodity price declines, is the best balanced in Latin America, and no longer dependent on the export of one or two raw materials. Tourists; remittances from migrant farm workers in the United States; and exports of cotton, coffee, manufactured goods, beef, sugar, shrimp, silver, copper, lead, zinc, chemicals, and oil make possible the imports needed for industrialization and have kept the peso stable for more than a decade. Sustained economic growth evidently follows upon political stability, to which it in turn contributes; workers and farmers are willing to abide by the system as long as it provides some concrete benefits and the hope of more in the future.

The key to the smooth functioning of Mexico's political and economic machinery is the regime's lack of ideology, except insofar as the vague concept of the Revolution itself can be called an ideology. Mexico's last five presidents, while differing widely among themselves, have all avoided such fixed ideas as the hardline free-enterprise policies of Argentina's Alsogaray and Peru's Prado, or the primitive Marxism of Cuba's Che Guevara. *Nacional Financiera,* a government agency, is a dominant force in the economy, currently contributing about a third of the new investment. Yet in recent years Mexico has become almost as attractive to United States and European investors as it was in the days of Don Porfirio; between 1945 and 1960 foreign investment tripled, and now totals more than $2 billion. And despite their evident successes, Mexico's leaders have none of the megalomaniacal dreams of Juan Perón or Fidel Castro; President López Mateos has repeatedly told reporters that "we do not seek the leadership of Latin America."

Under López Mateos, who announced in his inaugural address that his government would be "of the extreme left, within the constitution," the same pragmatic path toward revolutionary goals has been followed. The new President cracked down on politically motivated strikes by the Communist-dominated teachers' and railroad workers' unions—and then pushed through a compulsory profit-sharing plan for private industry. He nationalized the holdings of American & Foreign Power—and paid for them by borrowing from the Prudential Insurance Company. He has used federal troops against "parachutists," peasants who seize land without legal authority—but has stepped up the agrarian reform to an average of 4 million acres a year, the highest total since Cárdenas. In the 1962 budget, expenditures for education ($205 million, 21 percent) and social welfare ($137 million, 14 percent) reached new highs, while military appropriations $100 million, 10 percent) continued to be among the lowest in the hemisphere. Attacks on the President by left-wingers who want Castro-style expropriations and by the Mexican Chamber of Commerce, which deplores his "anti-business attitude," are perhaps the best measure of his success in sticking to an effective policy of moderate reform.

Mexico's position as the most advanced Latin American state naturally raises the question of how solid her prosperity is, and how feasible it is going to be for her Southern neighbors to follow the same course. It is apparent that Mexico's proximity to the United States, which has often plagued her in the past, gives her certain advantages today. Despite the development of native industry (steel production up from 1 to 2.6 million tons between 1959 and 1962, for example) her two major sources of income, tourists and the *braceros* (migrant workers), continue to depend on a nearby and prosperous United States. Tourism, the "industry without smokestacks," has in recent years brought about 800,000 Americans and $700 million in revenues to Mexico; it represents more than two-fifths of the nation's foreign exchange earnings. And Mexican migrant laborers, who totalled a record 440,000 in 1959 (plus a large number of illegal "wetbacks"), have brought back as much as $100 million a year despite wages of only 60 cents to $1 an hour. There is also much commuting across the border; one-sixth of the working population of Ciudad Juárez crosses to jobs in El Paso every day. Without these sources of foreign exchange, which are not available to other, more distant Latin nations, Mexico's economic situation would be much less favorable than it is. On the other hand, with three-fifths of Mexico's exports going to the United States, the nation is highly susceptible to increased tariffs, lowered import quotas, and dips in the United States business cycle.

Despite the rapid economic growth of the last two decades, Mexico is still a poor country and one in which wealth is poorly distributed; the current minimum wage is only $1.40 a day, and not everybody gets it. A 1960 study directed by Ana Maria Flores in the Federal District revealed the following income levels in one of the wealthiest parts of the nation:

Number of Familes	Family Income (monthly)
215,000	$40 and below
332,000	$40–$80
223,000	$80–$160
74,000	$160–$240
85,000	$240 and over

In the fairly typical state of Aguascalientes, half the population never eat eggs, butter, cheese, margarine, fruit, or soft drinks, and 90 percent never eat fresh fish, bread, or vegetables; some 10,000 families have an income of less than $16 a month. Even in Baja California, whose proximity to the United States makes it the most prosperous state in Mexico, the average family income is only $160 a month. The still pitifully small purchasing power of the average Mexican limits industrial growth by inhibiting effective demand for consumer goods; it leads to such anomalies as a shoe industry operating at less than half of capacity in a

nation where five million people go barefoot. As President Ruiz
Cortines sadly admitted in his annual report to the nation in 1956:

Yes, we have made progress; but the progress obtained by the country
as a whole enables us to see with greater clarity those who have still
not benefited by this progress. . . . I think, with much emotion, of
the great masses who are still suffering ignorance, illness and poverty.
. . . So long as these great masses do not progress at the same pace
as the rest of the country, we will have to say to those who are satisfied
with the present situation, "We have done very little indeed, the
essential promise has yet to be fulfilled."

Even more serious than the lopsided distribution of income,
which could be corrected by taxation and social welfare policies,
is the nation's unresolved population problem. Mexico's crude
birth rate is 4.7 children per 100 people per year, double that of
the United States and one of the highest in the world. Despite
a still tragically high rate of infant mortality (three times that in
the United States), the population has been increasing recently
by 3.5 percent a year, from 25.8 million in 1950 to nearly 35 million in the 1960 census. In a bad year like 1961, this booming
increase swallows up all the nation's increased production. And
Mexico, despite her large size on the map, has little available
farmland to provide food for the additional inhabitants she must
feed at current rates of increase. It is this unrelenting pressure
on the land that has led to the forced growth of the Federal
District (4.8 million people in 1960, one-seventh of the nation's
population) and to the movement of hundreds of thousands of
braceros across the border every year. The meaning of these
statistics in personal terms can be seen in the life of Oscar Lewis'
Jesus Sanchez, with his two dead and ten living children, and his
wistful remark that

They all need shoes right now. My other two little ones need clothes,
money for a doctor, for medicine. Delila is pregnant again. If I had
money I would like to have her operated. . . . so that she cannot
have more children.

Mexico's post-revolutionary regime, then, has managed to find reasonable solutions to the problems of political order, civil liberty, and overall economic growth; it has yet to provide a full measure of economic justice, and to confront the issue of unrestrained population increases. For Americans, the Mexican Revolution provides valuable lessons in the kinds of situations we are likely to face when other Latin American nations follow similar revolutionary paths. During the half century that has passed since the overthrow of Díaz, the United States has used various approaches to Mexico's revolutionary governments: diplomatic hostility, armed intervention, economic pressure, and the policy of the Good Neighbor. We now have enough perspective and enough analysis to see which policies have worked and which have not; if we use our Mexican experience wisely, we may avoid, elsewhere, some of the troubles we are now encountering in Cuba.

When the Revolution broke out in 1910, the new American Ambassador was Henry Lane Wilson, a Republican politician and a firm believer in the Divine Right of foreign capital. For Wilson, Madero's modest gestures toward reform amounted to "confiscation, harassment, and dislodgement through suborned judicial decrees"; he did his best to discredit the new regime, whose chances of survival he unjustly described as "hopeless." Acting in defiance of his instructions, the American envoy openly intervened to bring about Madero's fall and the assumption of power by General Huerta, whom he then formally presented to the assembled diplomatic corps. With the ambassador's tacit consent, Madero was shot a few days later; this incident was only one of many in Latin America in which American diplomats threw their weight against a popular regime and in favor of a pro-business, pro-American dictatorship.

After Woodrow Wilson's inauguration in 1913, American policy completely reversed itself, as far as support of Huerta was concerned. An idealist, with an inadequate understanding of Mexican reality, Wilson expected that nation to behave like her northern neighbor and to install a stable, democratic, responsible government as soon as possible. Breaking with the usual practice of establishing diplomatic relations with any *de facto* government, Wilson withheld recognition from the "illegitimate" Huerta regime; his purpose, he told a visiting European, was "to teach the South American republics to elect good men." This precedent, like the one set by Ambassador Wilson, was to return to plague us; we have currently put the Castro government in Cuba (as well as Mao's China) in a Wilsonian deepfreeze, without achieving anything worthwhile thereby.

Wilson, like Presidents Eisenhower and Kennedy after him, discovered that getting rid of a Latin dictator without the use of armed force was no easy matter; Huerta, like Castro, seemed to gain in popularity as a result of American hostility. The occupation of Vera Cruz for seven months in 1914 as a result of an unauthorized ultimatum by a belligerent American admiral did not accomplish much except to confirm all classes of Mexicans in their fear and hatred of the *gringo* invaders. A year-long chase after Pancho Villa's band in 1916–1917 was equally fruitless. Mexican opinion was so outraged by these two incursions on the national territory that the German Foreign Ministry thought (mistakenly) that Mexico might be enticed into a military alliance against the United States. Adroit use of a captured German telegram to that effect by the British Foreign Office played a role in bringing about American entry into World War I. The specter of a hostile Mexico allied with Imperial Germany provided a foretaste of the present peril to American security from Fidel Castro's ties with the Communist *bloc*.

The war, and the failure of Wilson's policy of intervention, diverted his attention from Mexican matters; he refused to react to Carranza's overthrow and murder in 1920 as he had to Madero's seven years earlier. With Mexico and the United States controlled by the conservative, business-oriented regimes of Calles and Coolidge, and with the Revolution seemingly having run its course, reconciliation between the two nations at last became possible. Ambassador Dwight Morrow, a former Amherst College classmate of the President, and a partner in the banking firm of J. P. Morgan, used sympathy and persuasion where his predecessors had employed threats—and accomplished much more. A

Mexican Supreme Court ruling in 1927 temporarily settled the vexed question of ownership of subsoil rights in favor of the American oil companies; Morrow brought the decision about by close personal relations with Calles, and made it palatable by numerous acts of friendship and good will. By 1934 it seemed that the active phase of the Revolution, and with it the source of friction with the United States, was over.

Under Cárdenas, however, both the Revolution and the old disputes with the *Yanquis* came to life. The quickened pace of agrarian reform touched more and more American-owned property, and Secretary of State Cordell Hull ordered Ambassador Josephus Daniels to insist that expropriation proceedings be deferred until satisfactory arrangements were made for adequate and effective compensation to American owners. The same language was to be used, with as little effect, in American diplomatic communications to Cuba a quarter-century later. To have agreed to immediate payment at market value for expropriated properties would have meant slowing down or abandoning the Revolution, something that neither Cárdenas nor Castro was prepared to do. And in Mexico, as in Cuba, the final clash of ideas and wills came in the oil industry, controlled in both countries by American and British firms.

Cárdenas, beset with innumerable administrative problems, was not anxious to take on any new ones; he was doubtless sincere when he told Daniels in 1936 that he would not, for instance, endeavor to take over the oil fields or the mines. But the oil companies, convinced that the industry could not operate without their sources of capital, machinery, tankers, markets, and technicians, presumed too much on their supposed invulnerability. They were unwilling to reach a new wage agreement with their Mexican workers, refused to accept a settlement handed down by the government Board of Conciliation and Arbitration, and finally defied the Mexican Supreme Court by announcing that they were "unable to put (its) award into effect." Three days later, on March 18, 1938, Cárdenas took over their properties.

Standard Oil of New Jersey, Shell, and the other companies responded with the same tactics they later used against Castro.

British and American tankers were withdrawn from Mexican ports, lawsuits against European purchasers of Mexican oil were instituted, an informal embargo of oil machinery was put into effect, and the American government was persuaded to suspend the purchase of Mexican silver (temporarily) and Mexican fuel oil for the United States Navy (until 1942). A flood of company-financed propaganda pictured Mexico as a nation in chaos, about to confiscate all private property and establish a Soviet state; service station attendants warned American motorists not to risk their automobiles—or their lives!—on a trip below the Rio Grande. Britain goaded Cárdenas into breaking relations, and Secretary Hull was restrained from doing the same thing only by Ambassador Daniels' "clearly insubordinate" insistence on watering down State Department protests. As Hull complained to a fellow Cabinet member, "Daniels is down there taking sides with the Mexican Government and I have to deal with these Communists down there and enforce international law." Looking back at the oil controversy with the perspective of twenty-five years and the additional experience of the Cuban Revolution, it seems obvious that we were fortunate to have an Ambassador "down there taking sides with the Mexican government"; and, by the same token, tragic that we have had nobody as wise and patient as Daniels in Havana during the past decade.

Because Daniels' shrewd but easygoing diplomacy turned out so well, and because it provides such useful lessons for the future, his handling of the oil crisis is worth considering in some detail. The Ambassador's preparation for his important post certainly did not seem auspicious. He was seventy years old, a political appointee, "not wealthy by the usual standards governing diplomatic appointments," and unable to speak a word of Spanish. Worst of all, he was remembered in Mexico as the Secretary of the Navy who had ordered the occupation of Vera Cruz twenty years before.

Far outweighing these theoretical drawbacks, however, were Daniels' personal warmth, his unpretentiousness, and his sympathy with the goals of the Mexican Revolution. Furthermore, as a personal friend (and former superior) of President Roosevelt, Daniels could communicate directly with the White House, and shape policy far more readily than any career diplomat. His intelligent comments on Mexican-American relations, reported by E. David Cronon in *Josephus Daniels in Mexico* (1960), can serve as a guide to how we ought to deal with future revolutionary regimes—and as a melancholy reminder of how we failed to deal with the one now governing Cuba:

Having made big money on absurdly low wages from the time the oil gushers made Doheny and Pearson rich, all oil producers oppose any change in taxes and wages, and resent it if their Governments do not take their point of view. Mexico can never prosper on low wages and we must be in sympathy with every just demand.

I think that with any kind of sympathetic, intelligent treatment, we may be able to help them pull through and have a friendly neighbor to the south of us. And I think it's terribly important to keep the continents of North and South America from going Fascist.

The oil and other big interests here have no sympathy with the good neighbor policy. . . . They go to bed every night wishing that Díaz were back in power and we carried the Big Stick and had Marines ready to land at their beck and call . . . I wonder at the ineptness of the representatives of the oil companies who are their spokesmen here. Some of them are so dumb that if they had to start a business of their own it would be foredoomed to failure. Initiative and tact are not in their vocabulary.

I believe every possible step should be taken to prevent the threatened break in relations between the two countries. . . . We are strong, Mexico is weak. It is always noble in the strong to be generous and generous and generous.

Patience is the virtue essential in a Good Neighbor policy. . . . These conditions call on our part for Patience, and more Patience, and Persistence and more Persistence, toward just agreements, even though such a course results in severe criticism from these who want the application of force.

It is certain that Cárdenas could not be ousted from office unless the opposition were supplied with arms by powerful interests, and that if that happened it would be the worst crime that has occurred in the Western Hemisphere since the days of Huerta. . . . We could bring pressure to bear by refusal to buy silver, but that would hurt the American owners of the silver mines, thus reducing employment here with consequent suffering to the worker, and would be deeply resented as a Big Stick measure. We could encourage revolution by permitting the import of arms by those who would wish to oust Cárdenas by force, with the consequent responsibility for the blood that would be shed; we could refuse to buy anything from Mexico, boycott its exports, and thereby reduce the necessities of life to the masses; we could denounce the country as dishonest and do much to strangle her; we could conquer it and put in a man as President who would be beholden to us; we could, after we had conquered it, make it a province or annex it and admit Mexican States to the union. We could do any or all of these things, but what would be the result? The Good Neighbor policy, the brightest hope of the Roosevelt Administration, would receive a body blow, and the people who are on our nearest southern boundaries would regard us as imperialists and oppressors, and many Americans would be grieved that we had returned to what they would characterize the Big Stick and Dollar Diplomacy, which were execrated when practiced by former administrations.

What a pity that the energetic and erudite young men who helped fashion President Kennedy's Cuban policy have never read or have failed to understand this useful advice!

Although the Daniels–Roosevelt policy of conciliation was opposed (and partially thwarted) by Secretary Hull and the oil companies, common sense and compromise won out in the end. Mexico did encounter great difficulties in operating the oil industry in the face of American hostility; new drilling ceased, production and exports fell, wages quadrupled, and production per man dropped alarmingly. But *Petroleos Mexicanos* (Pemex), for all its inefficiency and mismanagement, had become a source of intense national pride, and March 18, the anniversary of the expropriation, was celebrated as a kind of second Independence Day. After the war, when the feud with the American companies was patched up and President Alemán could afford to bring oil workers' wages back into line, Pemex became a well-run and profitable segment of the economy. Production in 1962 was over three times what it had been in 1938, and the Company's credit rating and technical proficiency today are excellent; it is even able, for example, to extend itself overseas to aid the Bolivian government's oil company in exploration, pipeline laying, and the export of crude.

The oil companies, in the end, had to give up hope of frightening, eliminating, or outlasting Cárdenas. Daniels remained in Mexico City, and the suspension of silver purchases lasted only a few days. As for the oil boycott and oil machinery embargo, Pemex survived them by selling a third of its oil exports to Germany in return for needed equipment. Ideology aside, Mexico was forced to deal with the fascist countries in order to survive American pressures, just as Cuba's revolutionary regime had to go to the Soviet Union for aid when the United States decided, as one official put it, "to let Castro's Government go through the wringer." Mexican-American relations, fortunately, were never allowed to deteriorate that far; a few weeks before Pearl Harbor a general agreement on the items in dispute between the two nations was reached. Mexico promised to pay $40 million for the agrarian claims and $24 million for the expropriated oil properties over a twenty-year period; the last payments were made in 1962. The companies had originally valued their holdings (including absurdly over-valued equipment and unpumped oil in the ground) at nearly twenty times as much.

The benefits to the United States of its policy of forebearance in the oil dispute were immediate, immense, and long-lasting. Even before Pearl Harbor Mexico was an active ally in hemispheric defense. Ávila Camacho broke relations with Japan on December 8, 1941, and declared war on the Axis powers five months later. The Inter-American Conference at Chapultepec Castle in 1945 confirmed Mexico's ties with the United States and her leading role among the Latin American nations.

With post-Cárdenas Mexico, then, the United States has developed an understanding as solid as those which bind us to such older allies as Canada and Britain. Disagreements—over the treatment of *braceros,* a boundary dispute in El Paso, the use of Colorado River water for irrigation, Mexico's continuing recognition of Castro's Cuba—continue to occur, as they always will between neighboring and sovereign nations. Mexico is an ally, and not a Banana Republic hitched to the American Empire. Yet López Mateos can declare, as Mexican Presidents before Cárdenas would not have believed or dared to say if they did believe it, that "cordial friendship with . . . the United States is a basic element in Mexico's foreign policy." It is evidently possible for a Latin American country to rebel against its helplessness and poverty, to take its destiny in its own hands, to forge out of error, confusion, injustice, and bloodshed, a modern state which provides a better life for its people and promises still more to them in the future—and to draw closer to the United States as a result. Older forms of government which leave the majority of the population outside the nation's political life are on the way out in Latin America, as in the rest of the underdeveloped world. Revolutions are clearly coming. And the question of whether they will follow the Cuban or the Mexican path depends to a considerable extent on the flexibility, the patience, and the wisdom of American policy during the next decades.

If the present state of Mexican-American relations, symbolized by the roaring welcome given the Kennedy's when they visited Mexico City in 1962, is cause for optimism, the continuing poverty of a majority of that nation's people must give us pause. If Mexico, the most advanced nation in Latin America, with the special advantages rising from her proximity to the United States, remains so poor, the outlook for the rest of Latin America must be bleak indeed. As Oscar Lewis sums up the present situation:

In 1960, over 60 percent of the population are still ill fed, ill clothed, and ill housed, over 40 percent are illiterate, and some 45 percent of the nation's children are not being schooled. The national wealth has greatly increased since 1940, but the disparity between rich and poor is even more striking than before, despite some rise in the general standard of living.

Under the Alliance for Progress we have undertaken to help change this sorry state of things, not only in Mexico but throughout the rest of Latin America. Let us see how a large-scale American aid program has worked in practice in Bolivia, one of the few Latin countries where it has been tried.

CHAPTER 8

Bolivia: Test Case for the Alianza

The U.S. and Bolivia have fallen into a double error of judgment. They have underestimated the profound nature of the social changes that follow the emergence of the campesinos *from their previous status as serfs, changes that will make social and economic institutions unstable for a long time. And both parties have overestimated what an aid program, even one of the broadest in the world, can accomplish in imposing stability on an inherently revolutionary process of change.*
    Richard W. Patch,
    "Bolivia: U.S. Assistance in a Revolutionary Setting,"
Social Change in Latin America Today (1960)

Bolivia's history provides a case study, exaggerated almost to caricature, of the reasons for the economic and political backwardness of Latin America. Geographic poverty, the heritage from Spain, a one-crop economy, racial and social tensions, and the absence of a middle class—conditions present everywhere to the south of us—are so overwhelming in Bolivia that one almost despairs of ever bringing the nation into the twentieth century. Yet this bitterly poor nation of only 3.5 million people (two-thirds of them illiterate Indians who cannot speak Spanish) celebrated in 1963 the eleventh anniversary of a genuine social revolution, one of the few to take place in this hemisphere. The significance of this revolution is enhanced by Bolivia's key position in the heart of South America, by its relation with similar revolutionary movements elsewhere in the area, and by its close

126

ties with the United States, all of which make Bolivia a proving ground for the concepts of the Alliance for Progress.

During the colonial period Upper Peru, as it was then called, was a source of immense wealth; the mountain of Potosí alone yielded 60 million troy pounds of silver (worth $600 million today), and the city of Potosí was the largest in all the Americas. The silver boom was followed, after a long interval, by a boom in other metals, especially tin. Bolivia also has large, though still unexploited, oil reserves, and the eastern provinces of Beni and Santa Cruz can produce cattle, cotton, sugar, rubber, and tropical fruits.

These promising prospects, however, have so far been illusory. Mining in Bolivia has always been a robber industry which rested on semi-servile labor and brought wealth only to a very few. And agriculture, which still accounts for two-thirds of the labor force, makes use of only 2 per cent of the land area, and that in the bleak *altiplano*, the two and one-half mile high tableland where the Indian majority is at home. Thus a nation the size of Texas and California combined, with a population density of only eight persons per square mile, the lowest in the hemisphere, cannot feed its own people. The *average* daily diet is estimated at 1800 calories. Bolivia imports more than half of its food and its per capita income of about $70 a year is, next to Haiti's, the lowest in the hemisphere.

Poverty-stricken nations paradoxically produce some of the world's great fortunes. A feudal system brought over from Spain and grafted onto the communal agriculture of the Inca survived in Bolivia down to the 1952 Revolution; the Indian tenant owed personal service to his master, and could be rented out or sold with the estate. A few thousand landowners thus lived in comfortable, though land-poor luxury, while their *pongos* (serfs) subsisted on a diet of 1200 calories a day and endlessly chewed coca leaves to deaden their hunger and fatigue. But the really big profits went to the tin mining companies controlled by the Patiño, Hochschild, and Aramayo families, which together produced 80 per cent of Bolivia's tin and 20 per cent of the world supply. Simón I. Patiño, an Indian from Cochabamba, came to control half of the nation's tin production and lived in Paris, Nice, and Biarritz like a great lord. His income, tax free because he was a Bolivian diplomat, was in some years greater than the national budget, and he once loftily told an inquiring official that he "was not interested in investments in Bolivia." Instead he used his immense income to purchase tin mines in Malaya and smelters in Europe, helping to decapitalize an already impoverished economy. The miners, subject to silicosis and tuberculosis and earning in most cases less than sixty cents a day, were kept at work by cruelly repressive measures punctuated by open massacres.

This iniquitous system was brought to an end by the triumph of the National Revolutionary Movement (MNR) in 1952. An armed MNR revolt defeated the regular army and brought Víctor Paz Estenssoro, a quiet-spoken former professor of economics, to power. During his first term (1952–1956) Paz transformed Bolivian society. The army was tamed by demotions, exile, and jail, and its weapons turned over to militia regiments of miners and farmers. Six months after taking office Paz nationalized the Big Three mining companies, promising, however, to pay for them at some time in the future. At the same time an MNR-sponsored *Grand Peur* swept the countryside; landlords and *mayordomos* were frightened off or driven off, and the Indians seized the land. An agrarian reform law issued by presidential decree on August 2, 1953 gave a color of legality to what had already taken place, and promised to pay for expropriated land with 25-year bonds (so far never issued). Although the actual granting of land titles was carried out very slowly (and with considerable violence and bribery of government officials) the number of people in landholding families shot up in a few years from 50,000 to 800,000.

The MNR Revolution, part of a continent-wide movement toward political and economic democracy, wrought a social transformation outstripping even the one that later took place in Cuba. Before 1952 the Quechua and Aymará Indians were not men but *pongos*, human livestock, who lived in wretched mud huts and slept on the floor like animals. The Indian majority was in the nation, but not part of it; it did not act, but was acted upon. As a recent Minister of Education put it:

The Indian is a sphinx. He inhabits a hermetic world, inaccessible to the white and the mestizo. . . . The Indian lives. The Indian acts and produces. The Indian does not allow himself to be understood, he doesn't desire communication. Retiring, silent, immutable, he inhabits a closed world. The Indian is an enigma.

The past decade has brought about greater changes than the preceding four centuries. Almost overnight the Indians were given land, the right to vote, military drill, and rifles. Peasants who formerly did not dare protest to their masters against forced labor of three or four days a week now come to La Paz to explain their problems to the President of the Republic, and receive a sympathetic hearing. In interviewing migrant sugar cane workers from various countries in northern Argentina a few years ago, I was struck by the superior sophistication of the Bolivians, who had formerly been the most backward. Mataco Indians from Argentina and Guaraní from Paraguay generally did not know their ages, what country they came from, or how much they were being paid. But the Toba, who came across the border from southern Bolivia in the harvest season, were well aware of their salaries, their rights under an Argentine-Bolivian labor compact, and the meaning of inflation and differential exchange rates. The awakening of the Indian population is the principal accomplishment of the MNR, and one which is spreading beyond Bolivia's borders to Argentina, Peru, and Ecuador.

This remarkable social achievement has, however, been put in jeopardy by the mediocre performance of the economy under the MNR. The text of the Agrarian Reform Law calls for the preservation of efficiently run medium-size holdings and the provision of technical aid to the new small holders. In practice, however, little distinction was made between badly-run *latifundia* and well-cultivated estates, and Bolivia lacked the technicians and the foreign exchange that would have made assistance to the peasant proprietor possible. Agricultural production, always insufficient to cover the country's needs, dropped rather sharply, and has yet to recover. Now master of his own land and labor, the Indian probably eats a little better and lives more comfortably, but he has neither the ability nor the incentive to produce a surplus for the market. This leaves the urban one-third of Bolivia's population more dependent than ever on imported food. As President Siles summed up the Agrarian Reform in his message to Congress of August 6, 1959:

The technical and economic transformation that has taken place is not the one the nation expects, desires, and needs. . . . Agricultural machinery has fallen into the hands of intermediaries or the large landowners of the eastern zone, not the peasant communities. Agricultural techniques have been organized on the highest levels without regard to the problems and interests of the poor peasant classes.

The agricultural slump was accompanied by a collapse in the tin industry. Since World War II tin exports had provided about two-thirds of Bolivia's meager foreign exchange earnings; in 1951, with prices rising as high as $1.80 a pound as a result of the Korean War, tin exports brought in $93 million. Shortly thereafter, for reasons having nothing to do with the MNR, the price fell as low as 80 cents, and until recently has hovered at about $1 a pound. Since each decline of 1 cent costs Bolivia over $600,000, this disastrous slide, typical of what has happened to other Latin American commodities such as coffee, wool, and copper, wrecked the nation's foreign exchange position at the very time that imports had become more essential than ever.

Even without the price decline the government mining company (COMIBOL) was in serious trouble. The former owners had put no capital into exploration or new equipment since about 1935, and the mines were in a run-down condition. Under government ownership things went from bad to worse. As a result of pressure from the powerful Miners' Union (FSTMB) thousands of new workers were hired and unproductive mines continued in operation; production nevertheless continued to slide, from

43,000 tons in 1945 to 30,000 tons in 1953, to 15,000 tons last year. Worn-out equipment, absenteeism, featherbedding, strikes, and depletion of the ore bodies have cut production per miner in half since nationalization. One director of COMIBOL negotiated a crooked contract for Argentine beef, escaped punishment and went off to comfortable exile in Buenos Aires; another was caught making profitable deals on behalf of the company with his parents. At present, despite a recovery in the market price of tin, COMIBOL's losses are running at about $1 million a month; it costs the company between $1.40 and $2.10 to produce a pound of tin that sells for $1.20. And hanging over the market is a United States strategic stockpile of 349,000 tons, part of which Senator Stuart Symington is now trying to have sold.

Given the chaotic state of mining and agriculture, Bolivia's revolutionary leaders would have faced disaster without American aid. And, in contrast to our attitude toward Castro's Cuba, such aid has been forthcoming, in an amount so far equal to about a quarter of a billion dollars. Although the free enterprise theology of Secretary Dulles led him to veto requested loans for COMIBOL and the government oil company (YPFB), he did approve shipments of surplus food, technical assistance missions, extensive road-building operations, educational and agricultural aid, and direct payments which have regularly provided between 30 and 40 per cent of the Bolivian national budget. In nine years our total aid has come to more than Bolivia's annual gross national product, and it is going to continue; Bolivia received the first loans under the Alliance for Progress. Our experience there thus provides useful information as to the expanded *Alianza's* prospects for success elsewhere in Latin America, and it must be confessed that the record to date is not a very heartening one.

To begin with, the program has been plagued with endemic mismanagement and corruption. Stanford University's *Hispanic American Report* (April, 1960, pp. 49–50) summarizes the findings of a Senate investigating committee:

It was discovered that no adequate financial records of expenditures or losses were kept until 1957, and that more than a million dollars were unaccounted for. Between 1954 and 1957 more than $2 million in food and fiber gifts were lost through overcrowding of ports serving Bolivia and theft of material in transit. Many expensive and ill-conceived projects were undertaken which later had to be abandoned because they did not suit the country's needs. A million dollars were wasted on a discontinued irrigation project in the Villamontes region of eastern Bolivia, which was so remote from populous areas that it could not be used. Two plants costing $225,000 to produce yucca flour would probably never be used, since there is no market in Bolivia for yucca flour. An agricultural vocational training center costing $160,000 was abandoned because it was too far in advance of Bolivia's needs. Agricultural equipment worth $500,000 was lost, and other equipment, including combines, was rusting in the original crates because, again, it was unsuited to Bolivian agriculture. Even the much-publicized powdered milk plant at Cochabamba, built as a joint U.S.-UNICEF project, was still not in production, and it did not appear that the plant would have adequate milk supplies for many years to come. . . . One confidential source pointed out that a sizeable percentage of U.S. aid had been diverted to the repayment of the Export-Import Bank loans so that the bank could maintain its record of no defaults. Another portion allegedly went for repayment of defaulted foreign loans which were contracted in the early part of this century under such scandalous terms that many do not think repayment should be resumed.

If we subtract these wasted sums and others like them, the total of our effective aid to Bolivia is somewhat less impressive. And American aid carried with it certain obligations. As Professor Robert J. Alexander points out in *The Bolivian National Revolution* (1958):

The United States was not willing to begin such a program until at least a preliminary arrangement had been made with the old tin-mining companies, in which a considerable amount of United States capital was invested. . . . Several years later United States advice was a key factor in the writing of a Petroleum Code which is, from the point of view of a foreign company seeking concessions, one of the most liberal in America.

Thus Simón Patiño's heir Antenor, who is so wealthy that he found it expedient to lend COMIBOL $5 million last year in return for a special divorce law, will continue to draw payments from wretched miners of the altiplano. And Patiño Mines, Incorporated (28 per cent United States–owned) continued to invest its Bolivian profits abroad, most recently in purchasing the Bowie racetrack and a luxury hotel in Mexico City. The spectacle of American money being used to buy new playthings for a multimillionaire is enlightening. Other American beneficiaries of "foreign" aid were the holders of $57 million in defaulted Bolivian bonds issued during the 1920's; MNR President Hernán Siles Zuazo, who succeeded Paz in office, was persuaded to resume payment on them in 1958. Grace steamship lines and the John Deere agricultural implements firm also profited considerably from our ICA program; and somebody evidently benefited from the United States surplus food shipments which found their way to the black market and thence to the Peruvian border.

As Professor Alexander suggests, the new petroleum legislation, written with the aid of United States experts, is generous. Bolivia nationalized her oil industry in 1937, and agreed to indemnify Standard Oil for its properties in 1942. But in 1956 the MNR agreed to grant forty-year concessions to foreign firms, along with special tax exemption and import permits. Professor Alexander's explanation of the circumstances surrounding this reversal of policy is worth quoting:

There was a certain amount of pressure exerted by the United States Government—or at least the Bolivian Government might well think that there was. In this connection the action of Henry Holland in resigning as Assistant Secretary of State for Latin American Affairs and turning up a few months later as a lawyer for oil interests seeking concessions in Bolivia has been criticized—particularly since he had been Assistant Secretary at the time the new Petroleum Code was written, with the help and advice of United States Government officials. . . . In the light of these circumstances, the Bolivians could not be blamed for regarding the sudden appearance of Mr. Holland so soon after his resignation from the top United States diplomatic post concerned with Latin American affairs as "pressure" of a rather obvious sort.

Private companies, with prospecting leases on 25 million acres, have so far spent $90 million in exploration and drilling; only one or two discovery wells have been successful, and these are in the isolated eastern province of Santa Cruz. Officials of Bolivian Gulf say that another $50 million in development will have to be spent before they can consider building a pipeline, and the present oversupply of Venezuelan, Middle Eastern, and Soviet oil on the world market make Bolivia's prospects dubious.

The American plan to encourage agricultural resettlement in Bolivia's empty eastern tropics, one of the few aid projects that has gone beyond the piecemeal, emergency stage, has also so far proved a disappointment. A 300-mile highway between Cochabamba and Santa Cruz was opened with much fanfare by Assistant Secretary Holland in 1954; when I visited Bolivia in 1959 it had been completely paved. The hope was that surplus farmers and miners could be attracted down from the altiplano and settled in farm colonies in the unexploited tropics. It was an attractive idea, and the mechanical engineering involved in building the road was superb. But the human engineering involved was faulty, for the Quechua and Aymará failed to behave like American frontiersmen excited by the prospect of cheap land. They had only recently gained title to the cold, windswept lands their ancestors had worked for centuries, and against all "logic" they refused to abandon them for new settlements in the jungle. Only a few thousand natives and some Japanese immigrants have taken advantage of the opportunity to emigrate, and many of them left after a year or two, disgusted with the strong-arm rule of Luis Sandoval Morón, the MNR boss of the area. Santa Cruz today still has fewer inhabitants than it had in the gaudy days of the pre-World War I rubber boom.

The result of Bolivian and American failure to come to grips with the nation's basic needs is painfully evident. No revolution in history has had so much outside aid, yet Bolivia's GNP fell from $210 million in 1950 ($84 per capita) to $191 million in 1961 ($64 per capita). The government continues to teeter on the edge of bankruptcy, and a murderous inflation has been slowed down but not stopped by an American-sponsored stabilization plan.

The Kennedy administration has given special attention to this inherited headache, which is such an ill omen for the success of our aid programs elsewhere. Spanish-speaking Benjamin Stephansky, formerly a labor specialist at the University of Chicago, has been named as our Ambassador in La Paz with the hope that a trained economist can suggest workable reforms. Kennedy has also been willing for the first time to make loans to state-owned industries, under new and more businesslike conditions. But it is already evident that we can still be pressured into loans and grants by invoking the specter of Communism and Castroism. American policy is still based on Professor Alexander's warning that the Communists "are the group most likely to profit from the national revolutionaries' failure"—a curious mirror image of the older argument that led us to support Pérez Jiménez, Rojas Pinilla, Rafael Trujillo, Fulgencio Batista, and every other non-Communist dictator in this hemisphere. This estimate is no doubt entirely right; but if the United States and the MNR cannot improve on their performance of the past decade, not even another $250 million will keep the Cubans, the Russians, and the Chinese out of La Paz.

Castro's plans for Bolivia are no secret. He has, of course, denounced the MNR leaders as "petty bourgeois, who have completed the surrender to Yankee imperialism"; on my visits to Cuba in 1960 and 1961 I kept meeting Bolivian Communist leaders who had been given paid visits to Havana to learn the techniques of propaganda and guerrilla warfare at the source. The Bolivian Communist party is very small—it received only 2 per cent of the vote in the 1960 presidential elections—but it has influence out of proportion to its numbers and is supported by a hyperactive Cuban embassy. Some local chapters of the tin-miners' union are Communist-dominated, and the Party has a voice in the central labor federation (COB). By calling for "direct action by the masses" for wage increases, such Party leaders as Ireneo Pimentel and Federico Escobar (both union officials at the big Siglo XX mine) hope to weaken the government and gain popularity for themselves. Professor Patch, on the scene in La Paz, reported in 1962 that "sentiment for Communist Cuba is a contained but explosive force." *Fidelista* influence was strong enough to make Bolivia one of the six nations that refused to vote for the expulsion of Cuba from the OAS at Punta del Este in 1962, despite enormous pressure from the American delegation.

The Soviet offensive in Bolivia has been conducted directly, as well as through native and Cuban intermediaries. In October, 1961, in New York Khrushchev offered $10 million to build a long-hoped-for tin smelter; in December a visiting squadron of Russian experts offered a $150 million low-interest long-term loan "without political conditions"—i.e., without even demanding the renewal of diplomatic relations between the two countries. Lincoln White, the State Department's press officer, has primly warned that a smelter "would be uneconomic and unfeasible for Bolivia at this time," and President Paz has so far hesitated to accept such a Greek gift for fear of losing his American grants— but he hasn't dared to reject Soviet offers outright, either. Late in 1962 the Bolivian Mining Bank signed a contract for a $1.6 million antimony smelting plant, to be financed and built by Czechoslovakia. Given Bolivia's desperate need for capital, similar contracts with other Communist nations may be expected in the future.

In Bolivia then, even more than elsewhere in Latin America, the cold war balance between the U.S.A. and the U.S.S.R. is a delicate one, and neither side has gained a definitive victory. No recital of the errors and shortcomings of the MNR and the American aid program should blind us to the accomplishments of the Bolivian revolution's first decade. The MNR made the Indian a part of society, and for the most part still retains his loyalty. It has provided that often-overlooked blessing, stable government; Paz, the first Bolivian president in thirty years to finish out his term, turned over the office in due course to Siles, and was in turn reelected in a reasonably free election in 1960.

As Walter Guevara Arze, the losing candidate that year put it, "a fraudulent election is better for Bolivia than a revolution." The MNR record on civil liberties is not perfect, but there are opposition newspapers and parties and deputies; the Chamber even went so far as to refuse to confirm ex-President Siles as Ambassador to Uruguay. Economic blunders have been made, but the record in Castro's Cuba does not suggest that Soviet-style development is any more rapid or free from error.

Our own mistakes, indeed, can be looked upon as part of our psychological capital in Latin America, as lessons in what is to be watched for and avoided in the future. We have rid ourselves of most of the inept amateur diplomats who got us into such a mess in Cuba and other countries. Kennedy's willingness to cooperate with socialism in Bolivia, Brazil, and elsewhere is a hopeful sign. So is the widespread success and acceptance of the Peace Corps, which is already active in Bolivia and bringing to bear the idealism and practical approach that has been lacking in the past. And, after all, no matter how troublesome and exasperating the job of trying to wrench a primitive Andean society into the modern world is, we cannot afford to abandon the effort. Cuba is an island which can be isolated and watched over, but Bolivia has land frontiers with other nations; a *fidelista* victory there would be a staggering defeat for democratic prospects in Latin America.

Facing the Future

Cuba is not an isolated case. We can still show our concern for liberty and our opposition to the status quo in our relations with the other Latin American dictators who now, or in the future, try to suppress their people's aspirations. And we can take the long-delayed positive measures that are required to enable the revolutionary wave sweeping Latin America to move through relatively peaceful channels and to be harnessed to the great constructive tasks at hand.

Senator John F. Kennedy,
The Strategy of Peace (1960)

One of America's less fortunate legacies from the last century is the illusion of omnipotence. After the Webster-Ashburton treaty of 1842, the United States enjoyed a singularly fortunate position in world affairs. With a friendly British Navy guarding the Atlantic reaches and a powerless Japan and China six thousand miles away across the Pacific, we were left free to pursue our Manifest Destiny in convenience and isolation. The only obstacles to our drive toward continental hegemony were the Indians, the Mexicans in Texas and California, the Russians in Alaska, and the Spanish in Cuba and Puerto Rico—all of whom were readily disposed of. By the end of the century we were prepared to announce, in Secretary Olney's splendid phrases, that

The United States is practically sovereign on this continent, and its fiat is law upon the subjects to which it confines its interposition. . . . Its infinite resources, combined with its isolated position render it

138

master of the situation and practically invulnerable as against any
or all other powers.

Times have changed, however. With the advent of *fidelismo,*
backed by a powerful Soviet *bloc* armed with nuclear weapons,
we are no longer absolute masters even in the Caribbean. So far,
at any rate, we have not been able to eliminate a hostile regime
in Cuba despite four years of strenuous effort. But old habits of
thought linger after the objective justification for them is gone;
during the 1962 crisis over Soviet missiles in Cuba dozens of
American politicians and editorial writers echoed Olney's mag-
niloquent boast:

Senator Capehart (Indiana) "The United States has every right to
    land troops, take possession of Havana, and occupy the country."

Representative Rivers (South Carolina) "It is as simple as the ABC's
    if you give the military the word to go ahead."

Spruille Braden (Former Assistant Secretary of State for Latin Amer-
    ican Affairs) "I favor . . . an all-out invasion by the United
    States Army, Navy, Air Corps, and Marines."

Time Magazine (September 21, 1962) "The only possibility that
    promises a quick end to Castro . . . is a direct U.S. invasion of
    Cuba, carried out with sufficient force to get the job done with
    surgical speed and efficiency."

Senator Engle (California) "We can take the top six feet off of all of
    Cuba with one air strike, and all that's built on it, and all that
    live on it."

President Kennedy, more realistic, and in a more responsible
position, recognized the limits of American power and refused
to wrap the Caribbean, and perhaps the world, in flames.

Any viable policy for Latin America as a whole must similarly
recognize the facts of economic and political power in the 1960's.
We cannot shape the destinies of the nations to the south of us by
military force, as we did during the earlier decades of this century.
The Guatemalan invasion of 1954, a belated return to the policies

of the Big Stick, was probably the last successful operation of its kind; even there we have achieved only an uneasy *status quo*, resting on a brutal and incompetent dictatorship. The principal lesson to be learned from our experiences with the Mexican, Bolivian, and Cuban revolutions is that intelligent diplomacy can achieve far more than military force.

If we must rid ourselves of our illusion of limitless power, we must also give up a more civilized and nobler notion—the idea that we can raise Latin America's standard of living to respectable levels within a decade or two by grants, loans, technical help, and exhortation. Secretary Dillon's promise that the *Alianza* would eliminate illiteracy, provide an improved water and sewer supply for 70 per cent of the urban population, and bring about "a minimum average rate of growth in income of 2.5 per cent per person in each country" seems impossibly optimistic at the end of the program's first two years. Teodoro Moscoso the *Alianza's* Puerto Rican director, has been more realistic. On the first anniversary of the signing of the charter at Punta del Este, he issued a memorandum referring to "spotty progress [and] . . . staggering and frustrating obstacles almost beyond endurance," and instructed his staff that the event was to be "marked" and not "celebrated"; "we will have time to celebrate when we have achieved an effective Alliance and made great progress."

The geographic conditions of Latin America, as mentioned earlier, are not likely to change. And ancient habits and attitudes like caudilloism, military dominance, lack of interest in science, technology, and agriculture, the absence of a strong middle class, and the white-Indian division will take, not decades, but generations to alter. Our own long and difficult experience with the Negro problem should stand as a warning to us against facile optimism about the ease of social change.

State Department spokesmen for the *Alianza*, glumly looking forward to their annual clash with Representative Otto Passman of the House Subcommittee on Foreign Operations, have tried to wring crumbs of comfort from current events to the south of us: the drafting of a ten-year development plan in Chile, the passage of a tax reform bill in Colombia, the adoption of a land reform scheme in Venezuela. But what magazine editors call "hard news" from Latin America has generally been bad:

The deposition and arrest of President Frondizi of Argentina, and the installation of a military regime.

The election of quasi-communist Cheddi Jagan in British Guiana.

Cancellation of the Peruvian elections and a takeover by a military *junta*.

The election of communist-supported Miguel Arrais as Governor of the populous northeastern State of Pernambuco, in Brazil.

Continuing (and increasingly harsh) dictatorial rule in Guatemala, Haiti, Nicaragua, and Paraguay.

Devaluation of the Chilean *escudo* and collapse in the value of the Brazilian *cruzeiro* and the Argentine *peso*.

Despite these discouraging portents, we are at least making a start. The Kennedy administration, for all its hesitancy and errors, has gone beyond the Eisenhower regime in recognizing the size of the problem that exists. While economic development in Latin America is not going to match our noble rhetoric about it, we can do much to encourage the process of change there. Rather than raking over once more the sins of John Foster Dulles or the blunders of the Central Intelligence Agency, let us suggest some policy changes with which most experienced observers of Latin American realities will agree.

1. We ought to stop talking about free trade and begin practicing it. Tariffs and import quotas imposed during the past eight years on copper, lead, zinc, crude oil, wool, long-staple cotton, fish, beef, and dairy products have severely damaged Latin American economies, cost United States consumers and businessmen millions of dollars, and deprived us of markets. Even coffee, grown nowhere in the United States, pays a three cents a pound tariff when imported in soluble form. Commodity exports provide a natural and healthy way to answer Latin America's desperate need for capital, and we ought not discourage them at the behest of special interests in this country. Some raw-material-producing

sectors of the American economy would suffer from increased competition, but exporters of machinery, chemicals, automobiles, and consumer goods would benefit. The Trade Expansion Act of 1962 increases the President's discretion in this field and will enable him, for example, to eliminate entirely duties on any tropical agricultural commodity or primary product provided the Common Market makes comparable reductions. It is to be hoped the President will use these new powers vigorously.

2. We need to do something about arriving at reasonable prices for Latin American commodity exports. Within the United States we long ago abandoned free markets. Yet the generally uncontrolled operation of supply and demand for tin, coffee, petroleum, lead, wool, and other Latin commodities is allowed to lead to disastrous cycles of boom-and-bust. Since the end of the Korean War, as the United Nation's Economic Commission for Latin America has repeatedly pointed out, the terms of trade have turned decisively against countries exporting raw materials. Latin American coffee, for example, brought in $2 billion in 1953, and only $1.5 billion in 1959, despite a higher sales volume, while imported machinery and consumer goods generally continued to cost more.

International agreements on sugar have been in effect for years, with reasonably good results; a new attempt to agree on coffee-exporting quotas seems to be working out fairly well. World prices will rise somewhat under similar arrangements for other commodities, but reductions in the American tariff would offset that rise. And increases of a few pennies a pound on a fairly narrow variety of imports will prove a lot less expensive to us than the collapse of a number of Latin economies and the subsequent spread of *fidelismo*.

3. We need better diplomatic representatives in Latin America—in President Kennedy's words, "the best men available." This is such an obvious truism that one hesitates to restate it. Yet it is clear that posts in Managua, Havana, Rio de Janeiro, etc., have often been considered excellent political capital with

which to pay off campaign promises. Business ambassadors like
Thomas E. Whelan in Nicaragua and Arthur Gardner and Earl
E. T. Smith in Cuba, who knew nothing about the countries to
which they were assigned and did not even speak Spanish, mis-
represent the United States and misinform the State Department.

There are no hard and fast rules for selecting successful
diplomats. Professional training and knowledge of Spanish or
Portuguese certainly seem desirable. But some Foreign Service
officers with long experience are stuffy and unimaginative, while
Josephus Daniels, despite his "impossible" background, did a
superb job for eight years as our Ambassador to Mexico. Despite
some shuffling and confusion in Washington, the Kennedy administration has notably improved the quality of our diplomatic
representation abroad with such appointments as Ben S. Stephansky, a labor specialist, to Bolivia; Lincoln Gordon, a Harvard
economist, to Brazil; and Raymond L. Telles, Spanish-speaking
former Mayor of El Paso, to Costa Rica.

To attract and hold such men, we ought to make some
changes in current diplomatic practice. President Kennedy has
been commendably zealous in protecting State Department employees against charges of "softness on Communism" that shat-
tered so many careers during the McCarthy-Dulles era. Another
needed reform is a substantial increase in ambassadorial salaries
and allowances, so that career officials and university specialists
can afford to take posts that at present must be reserved for
wealthy businessmen; Congressman J. J. Rooney's perennial campaign against "booze money for cookie-pushers" is ludicrously
against the national interest. It ought to be possible, on the other
hand, to reduce some of our oversized embassy staffs. It is hard
to believe that we really need five thousand people in Mexico
City—more than the number in the entire Mexican foreign office.
The current Foreign Service rules requiring rotation from one
post to another every few years should also be revised, so that
familiarity with the local conditions and language can be acquired.

Another obstacle to an effective Latin American policy is the
lack of coordination between overlapping agencies in Washington

and overseas. The State, Treasury, and War Departments, the CIA, the Agency for International Development, the U.S. Information Agency, the Inter-American Development Bank, our nineteen embassies with their health, agricultural, and military missions, the Peace Corps, and the Fulbright Commissions work independently of each other, and sometimes at cross purposes. Thus the Treasury may try to prop up the Argentine economy while the Department of Agriculture undermines it by banning canned beef imports and dumping subsidized wheat abroad; the International Monetary Fund may try to check inflation while the Pentagon is persuading the local military to buy some secondhand hardware. During Kennedy's first two years in office, key posts concerned with Latin American affairs have resembled a subway turnstile during a rush hour: A. A. Berle, Chester Bowles, Robert Cutler, Wymberley R. de Coerr, Allen Dulles, Richard Goodwin, Fowler Hamilton, Thomas C. Mann, Robert F. Woodward, and others, have hurriedly been shifted in and out of office; at least twenty men refused the post of Assistant Secretary of State for Inter-American affairs before someone could be found who would take it. The President has not yet found a man who can do for foreign policy what Secretary Robert McNamara has done for the Defense Department. In staffing the *Alianza,* meanwhile, we are overlooking some superbly qualified Latin Americans: José Figueres, who restored democratic rule to Costa Rica, Lleras Camargo, the deeply respected former President of Colombia, and Juscelino Kubitschek of Brazil, whose Operation Pan America was the source of the Alliance itself.

4. We ought, at long last, to put into practice Milton Eisenhower's 1958 slogan of "a handshake for dictators and an *abrazo* for democratically elected rulers." It is immoral—and shortsighted —to supply Latin dictators with United States tanks, machine guns, and training missions so that they can "fight communism." American ambassadors fawned on Batista and showered decorations on his generals, while the Pentagon gave his army $11 million worth of training and equipment. Yet Castro won, and rode

into Havana understandably convinced that the *Yanquis* were the enemies of his revolution. President Eisenhower paid no attention whatever to his brother's advice, and learned nothing from the Cuban debacle; during his last months in office Ike sent additional arms to Stroessner in Paraguay, maintained our Marine mission in Duvalier's Haiti, gave Trujillo 200,000 tons of the Cuban sugar quota, and sent an aircraft carrier and a squadron of destroyers to the Mosquito Coast at the request of Ydígoras and the Somoza brothers to quell a nonexistent invasion from Cuba.

The Kennedy administration's record is not much better. An assassin's bullet put an end to Trujillo's career, and we are backing away from our support of the Duvalier tyranny. But the remaining Caribbean *caudillos* are still courted for their votes in the Organization of American States and for their willingness to provide the bases from which we launched our invasion of Cuba in 1961. On his South American tour that year, Adlai Stevenson dutifully paid a call on General Stroessner, a ruler so brutal and incompetent that one-third of his nationals are living in exile. Our Military Assistance Program to Latin America has been increased from $54 million in fiscal 1961 to $64 million in fiscal 1962, and is going higher. Yet Acting Assistant Secretary of State Wymberley de Coerr still insists that there is "a growing tendency of the military to support constitutional rather than dictatorial governments, and to play a constructive rather than a repressive role within their countries"—a piece of wishful thinking rudely disproved by the Argentine and Peruvian army takeovers of 1962 and the 1963 *coup* in Guatemala. The military tradition is so entrenched in many Latin countries that it will not easily be rooted out. But we would do well to acquaint Latin officer trainees in this country with American democratic processes and with the constructive work of the Army Corps of Engineers, and encourage them to undertake similar projects of surveying, flood control, road building, and colonization at home. This would keep them employed and divert some of their budgets to useful purposes; they might even learn to prefer constructive work to *cuartelazos* (barracks revolts).

5. We can and should make a considerable contribution to Latin American educational progress. The job to be done is a large one, as the following UNESCO statistics indicate:

15 million children of primary school age (of 38 million) are not in school.

Of those who do attend primary school, only 1 in 7 reaches the sixth grade.

16.7 million children of secondary school age (of 20 million) are not in school.

There are only 600,000 students in Latin American universities (of a college age population of 17 million).

Latin America has only 50,000 engineers and technicians (as against 1.1 million in the United States).

Average schooling for all Latin Americans is two years; 50 million over fifteen years of age cannot read or write.

Embarrassingly enough, the largest programs for adult literacy, technical training, and universal primary education are in effect in Fidel Castro's Cuba. With their Literacy Brigades and "Year of Alphabetization" (1961), the Cubans took the lead over the rest of Latin America in the drive for mass education. Castro himself places such emphasis on education (and indoctrination) that he often takes part in the dedication of new schools, or makes speeches at graduation ceremonies; the newspapers, radio, and television cooperate in bringing the message of Marxism-Leninism-Fidelism from one end of the island to the other. Cuba's illiteracy rate is now one of the lowest in the hemisphere, and books pour off the presses in Havana in astonishing numbers. In a nation of seven million, for example, Blas Roca's tract *The Fundamentals of Socialism in Cuba* has been published in editions totaling 1.2 million copies, and is sold at a nominal price or given away.

Alianza officials, on the other hand, with less than $3 per capita per year to spend or lend, have made only a few grants for the construction of schools; they prefer to make loans for more directly practical things like water supply systems and sewers. In view of Latin America's tragically high infant mortality rate, this is understandable. But education would be a better investment, in the long run; an educated, prosperous community can build its own sewers. Our interests in Latin America would be better and more inexpensively served if we sent down thousands of schoolteachers and millions of textbooks, films, cheap radios, and other teaching aids in place of the aircraft carriers, jet airplanes, and instructors in guerrilla war we now ship south.

The improvement of primary and adult education, while an essential ingredient of economic progress, will take a long time to make its effects felt. A more direct impact can be made on the university level, often at trifling cost. A single professor of library science from the University of Illinois, on a Fulbright to Argentina a few years ago, did a great deal to improve the teaching of that unpretentious but vital subject. But the Fulbright program is too small to have sufficient impact: four grantees to Argentina in 1957, seven in 1958, six in 1959, five in 1960—as compared with the hundreds of army officers who travel both ways each year. And only seven of the twenty Latin republics have any Fulbright program at all.

Interchange of university students and professors could be stepped up at comparatively little cost; the gain in mutual understanding from such a program would be as valuable as the technical skills acquired. We should be aware, also, that the learning process would not be one-sided. While we are far ahead of the Latin Americans in most technical and practical subjects (there is not, for example, a single graduate school of agriculture anywhere south of the Rio Grande), they have much to teach us about literature, music, philosophy, race relations, modern architecture, and the art of enjoying life. Universities such as Stanford, Texas, Cornell, and Louisiana State have developed strong Latin American programs which could be expanded and transplanted elsewhere. Perhaps we might channel American help to half a dozen Latin institutions which could set standards for the rest. American businesses can also play an important role in providing on-the-job training and, in some places, in financing elementary and secondary schools. Government technical assistance and tax credits might encourage an expansion of these useful programs.

6. As the preceding item suggests, I think we are not spending enough money on our Latin American programs. The Alliance for Progress is often carelessly described as a "ten-year, $20 billion program," but a large part of that final figure melts away when closely scrutinized.

During the Alliance's first year the United States "committed" (but did not spend), $1 billion, 87 per cent of which was in the form of long-term development loans. Only $130 million was promised (but not spent), in the form of outright grants. This latter sum comes to about 65 cents per capita for its American donors and its Latin American recipients—hardly an amount adequate to fulfill President Kennedy's promise of "a vast cooperative effort, unparalleled in magnitude and nobility of purpose." The Alliance's appropriation for fiscal 1962 was only $600 million.

To calm the fears of fiscal conservatives who believe we are rather more than halfway to the poorhouse, it should be pointed out that we have already spent far greater sums of money in various ways which do not contribute much to strengthening our defenses, without ruining the economy. The now-useless DEW line, our expensive and soon-to-be-obsolete fleet of manned bombers, the wasteful rush to get to the moon before the Russians do—none of these kept Communism out of Cuba. Social progress through an adequate foreign aid program would clearly be less expensive and more effective than reliance on military force.

As evidence that we can afford to enlarge the *Alianza* program to adequate levels, some comparative statistics should be considered. In the spring of 1961 Under Secretary of State for Economic Affairs George Ball suggested 1 per cent of the national income as a reasonable amount to be set aside for aid to underdeveloped countries. We are a considerable way from that goal, and are, in fact, lagging behind two of our five major European allies in this respect:

Foreign Economic Aid and Defense Expenditures, 1961

	GNP per capita (in dollars)	Economic Aid per capita (in dollars)	Economic Aid per cent of GNP	Defense Expenditure per cent of GNP
United States	2823	19	.67	8.7
Germany	1438	10	.70	3.9
United Kingdom	1407	8	.59	6.7
France	1358	21	1.55	6.4
Italy	692	1.4	.20	3.6

[Christopher Willoughby, "Foreign Aid: Sharing the Burden," *The New Republic*, November 24, 1962.]

France is spending a great deal more, comparatively, on economic aid than we are, and Germany and England about as much; only Italy, with a per capita income on a level with Chile's and a major development program in her own south, is doing less. Yet the three Common Market nations on the list are enjoying full employment and such remarkable prosperity (double our own growth rate during the past decade) that President Kennedy has publicly wondered if we can't find out how they do it.

We might do well, *even as a defense measure,* to transfer some of our current Pentagon budget to the *Alianza.* A considerable part of our $52 billion military expenditure (1962) is frankly intended for pump-priming and cutting unemployment, as the Congressional stampede to force an additional $700 million into Secretary McNamara's unwilling hands for the RS-70 bomber program proves. Spending the money for books, machinery, trucks, bulldozers, structural steel and other equipment to be used in Latin America would be just as stimulating to depressed manufacturing areas, would bring future benefits in the form of increased trade (instead of becoming unsaleable junk in a few years), and might well prove to be the best, or even the only way to prevent Soviet expansion of their Cuban beachhead.

The following table of comparative prices will make clear some of the economic-for-military substitutions envisaged. When we consider that we have some $9 billion invested in Latin America (even after the Cuban expropriations), and that the area's strategic significance to our defense is incalculable, an increase in Alliance for Progress loans and grants seems only ordinary prudence.

Comparative Costs, Development Programs and Other United States Expenditures

Under $1 million:

Net development costs for the Cornell University project at Vicos, Peru	$ 5,000
Inter-American Center for Rural Education Budget (1963)	128,000
AID grant to University of Wisconsin to establish administrative training center (1962)	140,000
AID grant for 70 OAS Fellowships for study abroad	240,000
AID assistance program for Latin American trade unions	250,000
OAS Training and Studies Program for Agrarian Reform (1963)	380,000
AID loan to finance construction of 160 workers' homes in Honduras	400,000
Export-Import Bank loan to Ecuador to finance import of dairy and beef cattle	500,000
Pan American Foot-and-Mouth Disease Center Budget (1963)	600,000
Cost of fielding a three-platoon team in big-time football (*Fortune's* estimate)	750,000

$1 million to $10 million:

Inter-American Development Bank (IADB) loan to the University of San Marcos (Lima) to help establish a Department of Basic Sciences	$ 1.5 million
Fifteen OAS programs for Technical Cooperation (1963)	2.6

IADB loan for electric power program in Costa Rica	2.7
IADB loan to finance program of rural credit to low-income farmers in the Dominican Republic	3
IADB loan to help finance construction of 8500 low-cost homes in northeast Brazil	3.85
AID loan to Central American Bank to extend credit for agricultural and industrial development	5
New subway for members of the House of Representatives	6
IADB loan to expand water supply system in Maracaibo, Venezuela	6

$10 million to $100 million:

International Atomic Energy Agency budget (1962)	$ 11 million
IADB loan to finance expansion of electric power facilities in northeast Brazil	15
World Bank loan to Uruguay to rebuild main north-south highway to all-weather standards	18
IADB loan to finance colonization, housing, water supply and mining development projects in Bolivia	20
14 Canberra jet bombers purchased by Peru and Ecuador during border dispute, 1961	20
IADB loan to finance construction of 15,000 low-income housing units in Argentina	30
AID loan to Chilean National Development Corporation to help finance power, transportation, irrigation, housing, schools, and hospitals	40
Peace Corps budget, fiscal 1962	59
Aid to Cuban refugees in U. S. (1962)	70

$100 million to $1 billion:

Cigarette advertising on television	$100	million
U. S. losses on stockpile purchases of titanium	131	
U. S. military aid to Brazil, 1951–1961	180	
Rover nuclear rocket program (1962)	200	
Atomic Energy Commission decision to purchase surplus uranium ore, 1966–1970	200	
U. S. aid to Chiang Kai-shek government on Formosa	270	
U. S. annual expenditure on cold remedies	300	
U. S. annual expenditure on golf courses	350	
Grumman Aircraft contract to build moon vehicle	350	
Brazil's annual loss in export earnings, 1962 prices vs. 1953 prices	350	
World Bank loans to Latin America, fiscal 1961–1962	412	
One modern aircraft carrier (*Enterprise* class)	450	
Annual budget, Central Intelligence Agency (est.)	500	
Development costs of Skybolt missile (scrapped as inoperative)	500	
General Dynamics research contract to develop new supersonic fighter (1962–)	750	

$1 billion and over:

U. S. Department of Agriculture payments to reduce wheat and feed grains acreage, 1962	$ 1	billion
USDA annual cost for storage of farm surplus	1	
Total spent on education in Latin America, 1960	1.5	
Cost of funeral services in U. S. (average cost $940)	1.5	
U. S. aid program in Vietnam, 1954–1962	2	
Cost estimates for TFX supersonic fighter	2–4	

Gross National Product of six members of the Central American Common Market	2.2
NASA moon-flight program (fiscal 1963)	2.2
Total Latin American gold and dollar reserves, March, 1962	2.6
Annual U. S. expenditures on pet foods	3
U. S. imports from Latin America (1961)	3.29
U. S. exports to Latin America (1961)	3.33
U. S. economic aid to all underdeveloped countries, 1962	3.6
Annual Marshall Plan expenditures (90% grants), 1948–1951	4
Surplus in U. S. strategic stockpile, December 1962	4.6
U. S. financial aid to Republic of Korea (26 million people), 1950–1962	5
U. S. annual expenditure on cigarettes	7
Total value of materials in strategic stockpile (December, 1962)	7.7
Increase in U. S. military budget for fiscal 1963	8
Annual damages caused by U .S. highway accidents	8
Total stored farm surplus, 1962	10
Cost of U. S. program to send a man to the moon (est.)	20-30
U. S. Air Force budget, fiscal 1962	20
Gap between U. S. actual and potential output, 1962 (estimate by presidential adviser Walter Heller)	35
Latin American gross domestic product, 1962	65
Annual world expenditure on armaments	120
U. S. spending on military supplies and equipment, 1950–1960	250

Careful study of these figures is suggestive. I do not mean to imply that we ought to disband our army and navy, abandon our space program, slaughter all our dogs, cats, and parakeets, and stop smoking. But all our Alliance programs are concentrated on the upper, less significant section of the list; as Eduardo Haedo, former President of Uruguay's National Executive Council puts it, "The *Alianza* has degenerated into a program of using aspirin to cure cancer." We need to reexamine priorities and ask ourselves if this is really the way we want to spend our money; for "where your treasure is, there is your heart also." It should be noted that 5 per cent of the labor force and 15 per cent of productive capacity have been idle during the past few years for lack of effective demand. Since 80 per cent of foreign aid expenditures are spent for goods purchased in the United States, an increase in the program is indicated along purely Keynesian lines; the AFL-CIO estimates that some 700,000 jobs are currently dependent on such projects. Congressman Passman can afford to call the *Alianza* "a giveaway . . . a bottomless pit" because his rural Louisiana constituency is not interested in exports. But big-city Congressmen can be educated to call for *Alianza* appropriations instead of military spending as a stimulus to business back home. Resistance to an adequate foreign aid program would weaken if the American people were aware of how important Latin American markets, raw materials, and investment opportunities are to the American economy, and how close we are to losing more of them as we lost Cuba.

7. While the total amount of aid under the *Alianza* needs to be increased, and its duration extended beyond the scheduled ten years, we must also make sure that the money is used more effectively. Simon G. Hanson, an opponent of the whole concept of foreign aid, sarcastically points out that during the first year of the program the United States had:

. . . used some $200 million to bail out U.S. businessmen who had overextended themselves in Brazil and were now benefited by the Alliance in the form of retroactive cost-free insurance coverage; underwritten the largest single program of military-hardware purchases ever voted in Latin America ($280 million of equipment for the Argentine armed forces); made a campaign contribution of $150 million in a vain effort to hold President Frondizi in power against the wishes of the Argentine people; provided dollar-gap coverage for defaulted dollar bonds (Bolivian) which had been wholly repudiated by the President of the United States a generation before; [and] financed Colombia while the mounting corruption and the exfoliation of the bureaucracy . . . defeated hope for responsible economic activity in the public sector. [Simon G. Hanson, "The First Year: Economic," *Inter-American Affairs,* Summer, 1962.]

While this indictment of the *Alianza* as a mere "combination of political blackmail and shameless mendicancy" is overdrawn, the program has suffered a great deal from misdirected effort, mismanagement, corruption, and plain knavery. Underdeveloped areas naturally lack technicians, adequate planning agencies, and administrative élan; a crash program of economic aid is as sure to result in inefficiency and waste as a war is. We must, however, try to keep these to a reasonable minimum; as President Cárdenas of Mexico said, when told that his Cabinet officers were thieves, "Yes, they steal. But they steal with conscience and discretion."

What we need most of all is the courage to believe in our own rhetoric, and to deny aid to those countries unwilling to help themselves; as Senator Fulbright puts it, "If a country is not willing to make firm commitments for undertaking specific reforms, we should say that we are not interested." Among some Latin politicians and military men the *Alianza* is privately known as "the Castro plan"; one makes vague promises of reform, evokes the spectre of *fidelismo,* and collects soft loans and grants from Uncle Sam. To talk of an Alliance for Progress with the Argentine military, with the Somoza brothers, with Duvalier and other Caribbean oligarchs is absurd. Very little of the money we have been pumping into these nations ever trickles down to the wretched poor at the bottom of the social pyramid; instead, United States funds are used to enrich the already wealthy, and to strengthen the armed forces, the main prop of an unjust social order. A major turning point for the *Alianza* will come when military appropriations are cut back and economic handouts are refused on the ground that the recipient is not doing anything to earn them. After years of support we finally did cut off our aid to the Caribbean dictatorships of Trujillo and Duvalier, but the U.S. still actively backs military regimes in Guatemala, Nicaragua, Peru and Argentina.

8. Our aid ought to be channeled as much as possible to localities, and especially to the rural areas where more than half of Latin America's people still live. Most Latin countries suffer from an imbalance between their swollen capital cities, which usually dominate manufacturing and commerce as well as politics and administration, and their bitterly poor rural areas. In Peru, about one-tenth of the population lives in the capital, in Mexico one-eighth, in Chile and Cuba one-fifth, and one-third of the Argentinean population lives in Greater Buenos Aires. Aid pumped through these great metropolises tends to remain there, siphoned off by administrative costs, graft, and handouts of the kind Hanson describes.

We have, on the other hand, undertaken some highly successful ventures on the local level, the kind that public relations men like to call "People-to-People Programs." One outstandingly successful effort has been the transformation of the Vicos Hacienda in Peru from a population of mute and wretched Indians to a reasonably prosperous community, with schools, sewing machines, and a cash income of $20,000 a year. On September 1, 1962, the Indians purchased the land that for centuries their ancestors had worked for others—the first event of its kind in the history of Peru. Dr. Allan R. Holmberg, the Cornell anthropologist who directed the project, says he could now repeat it successfully "in a thousand other communities in from two to three years"; such an enterprise is well worth backing with Alliance funds. (The neighboring *hacendado*, characteristically, feels that the example of Vicos "is very dangerous. It could lead to a state of mind which could lead to an invasion of our haciendas." In 1961 he had the police shoot and kill three peasants who were planting potatoes on his land without permission.)

Another rural project from which we can learn a great deal is the Mexican system of rural education.

Having neither money nor trained personnel, the Ministry of Education resorted to sending "missionaries" on horseback to the villages in the mountains to preach the gospel of learning for the children. The villagers were gathered together and the difficulties and prospects were discussed in a kind of open assembly. It soon became apparent that the communities would build the schools themselves. The missionary turned architect, and the men, women, and children in their spare time and on Sundays and holidays gathered and hewed stones, mixed lime, worked the adobe, and built the school on land the community had given for the purpose. In a short time over 6,000 rural schools were built by the villagers without any cost to the central government, and having built them, the villagers felt as if the schools belonged to them. . . . The most important lesson that this movement taught was that there is a latent initiative and enthusiasm in the community that, once awakened, can be of great help in the development of rural education. [Frank Tannenbaum, *Ten Keys to Latin America*.]

But, as Professor Tannenbaum points out, half the children in the rural districts of Mexico are still without schools. Nowhere could American aid be used more effectively than in extending this kind of program in Mexico and elsewhere in Latin America; it would lead to an increase in agricultural output, it would make easier the location of light industry outside the swollen big cities, and it would help slow down the drift of unemployed rural workers to urban slums. The Peace Corps, which already has hundreds of volunteers at work on rural development projects in backwoods Bolivia, Brazil, Chile, Colombia, the Dominican Republic, and Venezuela, is admirably fitted for this kind of work; so are such independent undertakings as the Oakland County (Michigan)- Cali (Colombia) project sponsored by Congressman William Broomfield, the Inter-American Agricultural Promotion Service, and the hospital ship *Hope*, which brings new ideas and equipment to doctors and medical students in rural areas.

9. We must, as every publicist of the Alliance has endlessly repeated, encourage and support agrarian reform programs. Statistics for individual countries have been given in preceding chapters; for Latin America as a whole 2 per cent of the landholders own between two-thirds and three-quarters of all the agricultural land. One must visit, and preferably live for a while on some of these vast estates to understand how the hacienda system degrades the workers and militates against economic progress. On the sugar plantation of San Martín del Tabacal in Northern Argentina, for example, I discovered that only a handful of the 20,000 farm laborers employed at the peak of the harvest could read or write. The Mataco Indians who did the slow-paced subsidiary work of clearing out irrigation ditches, burning the trash left after the harvest, cutting wood and hauling it by oxcart to the furnaces, and topping plants, were paid fifteen cents an hour; their women, who did the planting and weeding, got nine cents. None of the children went to school, although the *ingenio* was legally required to provide one; when old enough, the children went to work for five cents an hour. With wages at these levels, the *patrón* had understandably little interest in purchasing machinery or applying scientific methods to his operation.

Sanitary conditions on this 100,000-acre estate were appalling. Permanent employees at Tabacal had solid, comfortable homes, and even the cane cutters were housed in passable wooden barracks. But the Indians were given only heaps of bamboo, straw, and sugar-cane stalks with which they constructed wretched little huts; the overseer told me that they preferred these, and that if they were given barracks they would burn them for firewood.

An even graver shortcoming was the company's failure to provide clean water for drinking and washing. The mill had an immense supply of pure water from deep wells for use in the refining process, but none of it was pumped to where the workers lived. On one lot the water supply came from a shallow uncovered well about thirty feet from a sewer-like irrigation ditch; on another, there was no pump at all, and the Indians drank from the ditch itself. In the fields, under a hot tropical sun, no drinking water was supplied, unless the Indians took the "precaution" of bringing their own. Diseases spread by drinking polluted water were naturally endemic; there had been no major epidemics, one exasperated government labor inspector told me, "only because God is great."

The *finca's* medical facilities for dealing with these diseases, and with the industrial accidents so common in a sugar mill, were also inadequate. There were only four doctors, eight nurses, and one ambulance to take care of some twenty-five thousand people, and the hospital was jammed from the beginning of the harvest to the end. The doctors explained that they found it unusual to examine an Indian without finding either intestinal trouble or venereal disease, but neither they nor the *patrón* felt it was their task to wipe out these scourges. The general feeling seemed to be that the Indians didn't mind getting sick, and that, anyway, they would only get reinfected after a cure. Meanwhile the mortality rate, especially among the children, was fearfully high, and two carpenters were kept busy full time making small coffins. "We don't charge anything for the *misa chica* or a plot in the burial ground," the *ingenio's* public relations man explained, "and they get the coffins at cost price." Yet conditions at Tabacal were considered good in comparison with those at the other twenty-nine mills in Argentina; a government accountant who regularly visits them all assured me that "Tabacal should be placed on a pedestal, and used as a model."

Such conditions breed *fidelismo* as a swamp breeds mosquitoes. The Coya, Chorote, and Mataco Indians I interviewed (with difficulty—many of them knew no Spanish) did not recognize the Argentine flag and had never heard of President Frondizi; but one of them solemnly assured me (in 1959) that "Fidel Castro was a friend of the Indians." In Havana in 1960, 1961, and 1962, I met Latin Americans from a dozen nations who had come to Cuba, as Raúl Castro put it, "to drink from the pure fountain of the Revolution," and to go home and spread the gospel; and the first commandment was always *la reforma agraria.*

In trying to forestall the violent methods of *fidelismo* and bring about an end to rural misery in a peaceful, democratic way, we must not let our indignation and enthusiasm outstrip our knowledge. The agrarian problem has a different aspect in different countries. In Bolivia, for example, all the large estates were broken up by the MNR revolution and distributed to the Indians—who promptly let production slide to a subsistence level. The highlands are overcrowded, but Bolivia has empty lands in the interior as do Peru, Venezuela, and Brazil; the great need here is for roads, bridges, technical assistance, and credit to start colonization projects. Breaking up Tabacal or the immense Argentine cattle ranches might even be a mistake, for sugar and beef production require large amounts of land to make the necessary capital investment feasible; what seems to be indicated is enforcement of existing laws concerning education, minimum wages, medical facilities, housing, sanitation, and revision of the tax laws to encourage the *patrón* to dispose of part of his property. It is more important to continue existing production, to encourage diversification and self-sufficiency, to increase total output, and to share the results more equitably than it is to apply dogmatically any fixed rule. Doctrinaire programs in agriculture usually fail; the Bolivian division of the land and the Cuban transformation of private estates into state-owned *granjas del pueblo* have so far resulted in decreases in production. In Haiti, the problem of the *hacienda* is reversed. The sugar plantations were broken up by Toussaint l'Ouverture and Jean Jacques Dessalines at the end of the eighteenth century, leaving a peasant society crowded onto tiny plots which grow smaller as they are divided by inheritance over the generations.

To cope with such a variety of agrarian problems, we should cooperate with Latin American governments in sponsoring a variety of solutions. The Department of Agriculture, the land-grant colleges, and various commercial organizations have transformed American agriculture by such discoveries as hybrid corn, fertilizers, insecticides, the Beltsville turkey, and commercial uses for peanuts, soy beans, and sugar-cane stalks. If they can make similar discoveries that could be applied to Latin America's tropical areas—cheap power for air conditioning, a way to

can mangoes or make banana flour or banana chips, for example
—millions of acres of presently useless land would become available for agricultural purposes. About half of South America falls
within the Amazon belt, and under present conditions it has a
population of only one person per square mile.

To dismiss the complex subject of agrarian reform in only a
few paragraphs is, of course, an impertinence. About the only
generalization that will stand up is that there are no generaliza-
tions worth making. We should, however, direct our financial and
technical assistance to agriculture, and insist that no government
which fails to make a determined effort to solve its farm problems
will receive help from us.

10. Closely related to the question of agrarian reform is the
even more difficult one of population control. In recent years the
population increase in Latin America has been running at about
2.6 per cent a year (as against 1.7 per cent for the United States),
despite an infant mortality rate three and four times that of the
United States. Every year, despite the death of 800,000 infants
less than one year old, there are five million more people to
feed and clothe and shelter. It is this rate of increase (which if
continued will lead to a Latin American population of 300 million in 1975 and 600 million by the end of the century) that
swallows up economic growth and that has held the increase in
per capita income to a little over 1 per cent a year since 1958.
While applauding *Alianza* programs designed to lower death
rates from polluted water and insect-borne disease, we must ask
ourselves if we are not simply permitting more people to survive and go hungry for the rest of their lives. As World Bank
President Eugene R. Black puts it, "We are coming to a situation
in which the optimist will be the man who thinks that present
living standards can be maintained."

A massive birth control campaign should doubtless have high
priority in any rational scheme for Latin America's future. A
1959 report drawn up by Presidential Special Adviser William H.
Draper recommends that the United States encourage such a

program, but political realism makes it plain that no American president is going to support it. Nor would Latin Americans themselves take kindly to any widely propagandized *Yanqui* scheme to limit their numbers; President Kennedy has correctly pointed out that "it would be the greatest psychological mistake for us to appear to advocate the limitation of the black or brown or yellow peoples whose population is multiplying no faster than that of the United States."

Nevertheless, the Puerto Rican experience, where the largest government-sponsored birth control program in the world has been put into effect against violent clerical opposition, suggests that there is strong latent interest in family limitation. The Family Planning Association in Puerto Rico operates counseling clinics, distributes free literature and contraceptive pills and has legally sterilized more than 100,000 men and women. One out of every four fertile married women on the island has received a supply of a contraceptive foam supplied free of charge by an American philanthropist. In Japan, legalized abortion and widespread use of contraceptives have cut the birth rate in half, from 3.4 per cent in 1948 to 1.7 per cent in 1960. Similar though less effective programs are being tried in mainland China, Egypt, India, South Korea, and elsewhere; Pakistan's President Mohammed Ayub Khan, calling birth control "our problem number one," has told Washington that "we look to you . . . to apply your mind and your resources . . . to this problem."

That the effort to reduce reproductive rates is not hopeless, even in underdeveloped and for the most part Catholic countries, can be seen in the fact that some Latin nations (Argentina, Bolivia, and Uruguay) already have birth rates below that of the United States (which may itself, perhaps, be producing too many children). Contraceptive devices have long been on sale in all of Latin America's big cities, and they are freely used to limit family size; the Chilean Ministry of Health has even appointed a commission to study the nation's high birth rate and to make recommendations for lowering it. The Roman Catholic Church itself, at the recent Ecumenical Council, gave some indication of increased willingness to countenance family limitation if not accomplished by "means that are against nature." Latin American Catholics, like those elsewhere, simply disregard their church's views when they have sufficient knowledge and financial ability to do so.

The world's underdeveloped areas will make little real economic progress unless they can somehow break out of the vicious circle in which large families cause poverty which in turn causes large families; "the poor man's table is miserable, but his bed is productive." As one United Nations official puts it, "Latin America cannot achieve a higher standard of living without birth control, but it cannot achieve birth control without a higher living standard." Movement up the income scale generally brings about a reduction in the birth rate; this process might be aided by programs sponsored by Latin governments and by such private American groups as the Planned Parenthood Federation. The greatest obstacle to widespread use of contraceptives in the backward areas of the world is their high cost; a year's supply of one well-known birth-control pill is currently $42, one-seventh of Latin America's per capita income. Continued research by the big pharmaceutical companies can reduce this figure, and our government might find it possible to subsidize a birth control program if it were initiated by a Latin government, and if our aid could be handled with sufficient discretion. Cheap and available contraceptives are part of the solution to the problem; another is better understanding of the social and cultural sources of oversized families as analyzed, for example, in J. Stycos' excellent study *Family and Fertility in Puerto Rico* (1955).

11. We need to do something to slow down the flight of private capital from Latin America. United States businessmen, responding to recessions at home, *fidelismo* in Cuba, threats of expropriation in a dozen other countries, and the greater safety and profitability of investment in Canada, England, and the Common Market, have decisively turned away from Latin America since the booming days of the early 1950's:

Inflow of United States Private Capital

1957	$1163 million
1958	299 million
1959	218 million
1960	95 million
1961	141 mililon
1962 (first 9 months)	49 million

Repatriated profits have been running at three or four times these sums; in 1959, for example, $775 million was sent to the United States. Latin Americans themselves have been steadily sending money abroad to havens in Wall Street, Switzerland, and Florida. Flight capital is by definition frightened capital, and much of it is sent abroad illegally, so that the total amount cannot accurately be determined. We do know that U.S. banks hold $2.5 billion in short-term Latin American liabilities. A Congressional subcommittee estimates that Latin Americans have a total of $10 billion abroad; *Visión*, the Mexican businessman's magazine, believes that it is more than $15 billion.

Fidelistas and doctrinaire socialists will argue that this mass getaway is all for the best, since private capital is only exploitative, and cannot build real prosperity. In point of fact, however, Latin America would be worse off than it is without the capital equipment, entrepreneurial skill, and technical knowledge brought in by the American companies. Corporations such as Creole, Kennecott, Grace, and United Fruit can undertake operations which are far beyond the abilities of native capitalists or governments, and exploit resources which would otherwise go untapped. They make large profits, but they generally pay good wages: Venezuelan oil workers enjoy a privileged position in the national economy, and get about as much, in wages and fringe benefits, as their counterparts back in the United States. Anaconda and Kennecott pay a Chilean copper miner with a wife and two children $19 a day in wages and fringe benefits such as free housing, hospitals, schools, and subsidized food; in addition, they provided three-quarters of Chile's foreign exchange and paid $74 million in taxes in 1961, one-fifth of the national budget. Chile has desperate social problems, but they spring from agricultural paralysis, bureaucracy, and the indigenous social order, not from the successful copper companies.

American (and Western European) corporations will not, of course, invest in an area beset by chronic instability and social unrest. They are willing, though naturally reluctant, to pay heavy taxes (the copper companies in Chile pay 70 to 80 per cent of their net profits to the government), but they must have some form of insurance against extraordinary risks. This may best be provided by inherent governmental stability and fairness, as in Uruguay or Mexico. Elsewhere, the Department of Commerce program of investment insurance may be effective, though the experiment is still too new to evaluate. Professor Frank Tannenbaum's suggestion that we secure fair payment for expropriated properties by placing a temporary repayment tax on imports from the country involved is worth consideration. It would act as a kind of automatic insurance policy, and smooth the way for transfer of properties to Latin American hands without disrupting normal relations. Franklin Roosevelt's successful handling of the Mexican oil expropriations provides a useful model for future problems of this kind.

In the long run, however, most of the big companies will be forced to alter the nature of their operation or to get out of Latin America entirely. The mining corporations and the utility holding companies are particularly liable to attack; they are so visible that nationalist politicians from one end of Latin America to another find them an easy target. The popularity of men as different in political style as Lázaro Cárdenas, Juan Perón, and Getulio Vargas was cemented by their programs for nationalizing basic industries; Fidel Castro's massive expropriations in the fall of 1960 were greeted by most of the Cuban people with genuine enthusiasm. The trend is continuing; during the past few years, for example, the Mexican government bought out American & Foreign Power, the Governor of Rio Grande do Sul in Brazil expropriated a subsidiary of International Telephone and Telegraph, and the Braden and Anaconda Copper Companies cancelled plans for $325 million in new investments because the Chilean Congress was unwilling to give them the guarantees they felt they needed.

Future United States investment in Latin America, then, seems likely to avoid such politically vulnerable sectors of the economy, to concentrate on the manufacture and sale of consumer goods, and to stay relatively small. The model for this newer kind of operation is Sears Roebuck, which began overseas operations in 1942 and now operates in five Latin countries. Acutely conscious of latent enmity to *Yanqui* businessmen, Sears has tried to become as closely identified with its workers, customers, and suppliers as possible. In Brazil and Colombia, for example, 99 per cent of the goods sold are purchased from local manufacturers, some of whom were started in business by Sears contracts, technical advisers, and financing. Three subsidiaries have profit-sharing plans; employees already own 13 per cent of the company in Venezuela and 20 per cent in Mexico. Of Sears' five thousand overseas employees in 1962, only forty-five were American citizens, and the company assiduously cultivates good will through scholarships, a free elementary school, manual training classrooms, and vacation camps for the underprivileged. An operation so thoroughly acclimated is in far less danger of political trouble than the old giants engaged in extractive industry or agriculture, and Sears' retailing innovations—inventory control, fixed prices, high turnover, handling of cash by sales persons— are spreading in all the cities where the firm has branches. The United Fruit Company, for decades a *bête noire* of Caribbean nationalists, is similarly selling its banana lands to native farmers and confining its activities to marketing, transportation, and the supply of agricultural technical services.

In their treatment of native capitalists, Latin governments can be encouraged to be more peremptory. The British economist Nicholas Kaldor has estimated that the upper classes in Chile pay only 15 per cent of their income in taxes, and spend over four times as much in nonproductive conspicuous consumption. Tax reform laws can channel some of this wealth into productive enterprises, just as revisions of the real estate tax structure could quietly do away with the outmoded *hacienda* system.

We cannot, of course, compel Latin legislators, most of them members of the wealthy classes, to vote away part of their privileged position in society. But we cannot prop up unpopular, outmoded governments forever, either. If a Latin regime is both undemocratic and unwilling to become so, we have no obligation to support it; we must find the courage to see it toppled by revolution and the skill to come to terms with the new order. We did this readily in Algeria, Egypt, and Indonesia, where little American investment was involved; we managed to do it with somewhat more difficulty in Mexico and Bolivia; we failed to do it at all in Cuba. Nothing could be more fatal to America's future than to let the Soviet *bloc* monopolize the social revolutions that are coming to so many nations in the southern half of the world.

12. We need to encourage the growth of a Latin American version of the Common Market. Seven of the twenty republics to the south of us have less than three million people; eight have from three to ten million; two have between ten and fifteen million; only Argentina (twenty-one million), Mexico (thirty-six million), and Brazil (sixty-nine million) are larger than that. Added together, all of Latin America has only about as many people as the United States and Canada, and it has, of course, a vastly smaller market for capital and consumer goods. The six Central American republics put together have a smaller population than New York or California and a combined annual income considerably less than that of any one of a dozen American cities. These fragments of the Spanish and Portuguese empires cannot develop modern economies inside their own restricted borders; they need to build a customs union and, later on, some form of supra-national economic authority.

Encouragingly enough, after a century and a half of talk, two regional economic groups are emerging. In its first few years the Central American Common Market (CAPEI) has eliminated barriers on about half the trade of the five member countries, standardized external tariffs on more than 80 per cent of all commodities, and set in motion machinery for resolving disputes between signatories of the 1958 treaty. The Latin American Free Trade Area (LAFTA), set in motion by the 1960 Treaty of Montevideo, now includes 150 million people in Argentina, Brazil, Chile, Colombia, Ecuador, Mexico, Panama, Peru, and Uruguay; Bolivia and Venezuela may be expected to join very shortly. LAFTA's potentialities can be estimated from the fact that Mexico increased its exports to member nations by 50 per cent in the year after the first tariff cut, and Uruguay doubled hers. The Inter-American Development Bank has deliberately channeled its loans into projects that have a multinational scope and that take advantage of the new regional markets. The most recent step taken by the Association has been the creation of a merchant fleet designed to save some of the $1.2 billion annually paid out to foreign shippers by LAFTA members.

If these regional plans go forward, and are eventually combined, they will provide an economic base for an already existing cultural unity. The wars of liberation which created the Latin American republics were not isolated struggles, but a continental effort; San Martín of Argentina and Bolívar of Venezuela are also heroes in Chile, Colombia, Ecuador, Peru, and Bolivia. These nations have similar unhappy histories, suffer the same social problems, are familiar with the same poets and philosophers; in a literal sense, they speak the same language. Economic union would open important new markets, expose the more backward nations to bracing new ideologies and competition, make possible a sizable scaling down of the current $2 billion arms budget and permit the release of some of the 650,000 men now under arms.

13. More of our aid should be multilateral and channeled through international agencies like the U.N. and the OAS. Bilateral agreements between the rich and the poor, between a strong nation and a weak one, invariably arouse resentment no matter how well-intentioned the Great Power may be. The *Alianza* is hotly denounced throughout Latin America by leftists as a new

disguise for "Yanqui imperialism" and by rightists as a Communist scheme to foment social revolutions. Many Latin Americans, with their Europe-oriented views of the United States, think of us as their cultural inferiors—dollar-chasing, Negro-baiting Anglo-Saxons. United Nations agencies, with their neutral viewpoint and experienced personnel, do not face these psychological handicaps; even Fidel Castro is able to get along with some of them. The United Nations is also able to secure additional funds from other advanced nations, and pool them for greater effectiveness. If we are really interested in economic development, and not merely in fostering anti-Communist sentiment, we ought to make more use of such superbly functioning organizations as the U.N.'s Technical Assistance Administration.

14. The U.S. must recognize Latin American independence, and deal with Latin nations on the basis of real equality. The decades of dollar diplomacy, of the Monroe Doctrine and the Big Stick, the years when an American Secretary of State could behave toward Latin American sheep as a shepherd—or as a wolf —are over. Secretary Dulles' performance at Caracas in 1954, when he insultingly left the conference after hammering through the anti-Guatemala resolution that he wanted, was the last of its kind. Since 1959 Cuba, once the most docile follower of American policy, has been taken over by an angry, defiant, and exasperatingly independent leader. Brazil and Mexico, to name only the largest of the new neutrals, have also struck out on independent lines. At the beginning of 1963, despite enormous American pressures, five nations with considerably more than half of Latin America's population (Bolivia, Brazil, Chile, Mexico, Uruguay), still maintained embassies in Havana and still hoped to bring Castro back into the hemispheric fold. An increasing number of Latin countries are trading with the Soviet Union, not for ideological reasons, but because they need markets for their sugar, coffee, copper, and wool (the U.S.S.R. bought three-fifths of the Uruguayan wool clip in 1960). We must act in the future by persuasion, and not by bribery or force. But some American politicians and diplomats still do not understand the new situation.

During the 1962 Cuban crisis, for example, Congressman Brown of Ohio expressed the old outmoded ideas:

Our troubles started back in the Franklin D. Roosevelt administration . . . when he entered into what was called the Good Neighbor policy. . . . That policy continued until, under Mr. Truman, we entered into the Organization of American States and agreed . . . that we would not decide for ourselves what we should do to protect American properties and American lives in any Latin American country. . . . For a good many years down in Latin America, on forty different occasions, American armed forces . . . moved into countries south of the border. . . . But lately we have adopted this namby-pamby policy of attempting to turn to Latin American countries, to ask their permission. [*Congressional Record,* September 25, 1962.]

Fidel Castro regularly quotes from such speeches and broadcasts them the length and breadth of Latin America to show that the Yankees haven't changed since the Bad Old Days of Dollar Diplomacy.

15. One of the major realities of the new Latin America which we will have to accept is a widespread preference for a managed economy and for some form of socialism. The habit of looking to the central government for action in the field of price-fixing, city planning, education, electrification, housing, mining, transportation, and general supervision of the economy (matters which are handled in the United States, for the most part, by private business and local authorities) goes back to the days of the conquest, when the Spanish monarchy played a dominant role in the economic life of the empire. Even today most Latin nations are so loosely held together that the central authorities must be strong if there is to be any unity at all; and even a right-wing businessman's government like President Alessandri's in Chile will undertake large socialistic schemes for electric power, coal mining, and railroad development.

Latin American governments, consequently, exercise a degree of control over the economy which Barry Goldwater or the NAM would consider tyrannous. Many Latin nations look with favor on a government oil monopoly; Pemex, Petrobras, and YPF (in Argentina) are highly popular institutions which politicians tamper with at their peril. Our long quarrel with Mexico focused on the oil industry; and one of the most unfortunate aspects of Eisenhower's foreign policy was his administration's devotion to the interests of American oil companies in such countries as Argentina, Guatemala, Venezuela, and Cuba.

The Latin dictators with whom we were so satisfied in the 1950's were eager, of course, to cooperate with American private enterprise as long as they got their share of the profits. But as governments with popular support come to power, they uniformly favor increased government control and ownership of basic industries. The massive Cuban expropriations are only an extreme example of a trend which is world-wide in scope. Nehru, Nkrumah, and Nasser are all agreed upon the need for government ownership or control of the economy; they are all leading their nations in a similar direction, though at different speeds and under different political conditions. Even in this country, as the clash between President Kennedy and United States Steel demonstrated, basic decisions over such a fundamental matter as the price of steel are not completely in the hands of private corporations.

We may, of course, have reservations about the wisdom of large-scale expropriations for most Latin American nations at the present time. The dismal record of state-operated Argentine railroads, Bolivian tin mines, and Cuban sugar plantations makes it clear that nationalization of industry is no panacea for economic ills. Political realism, moreover, requires Latin Americans to recognize that uncompensated seizures of American property will result in economic retaliation and the cutting off of United States aid. Such decisions, in any event, must be made by Latin countries themselves.

The United States government and our corporations must learn to live with the Latin preference for nationalized industries, mistaken as we may believe it to be. In this respect the Kennedy administration's willingness to make loans to Petrobras, and its cautious reaction to expropriations in various Brazilian states are notable improvements over the almost religious devotion to American corporate interests of John Foster Dulles. Perhaps we are at last beginning to understand, and to make it clear to Latin Americans, that we are not trying to save them *for* capitalism, but to save them *from* Soviet domination.

16. Such a reshaping of our foreign policy cannot be accomplished without considerable changes, some of them painful, within the United States. It was perhaps possible, in the old days of professional diplomacy for which George Kennan is so nostalgic, to conduct foreign policy without much reference to domestic affairs; British and French governments in the last century could be liberal at home and repressive in the colonies. But there have been revolutionary changes in communication, weapons systems, economic interdependence, and even tourism. We live in a shrinking world, in which "domestic" matters (Hitler's persecution of the Jews, the Spanish Civil War, Khrushchev's campaign against Stalinism, the Cuban revolution) are subjects of legitimate international concern. It has become impossible to draw a clear line between foreign and domestic policy: to improve our relations with Latin America we must manage to find solutions to some of our problems at home. If we can get the wobbly American economy back into high gear, for example (one out of every seven industrial workers is unemployed in the county in which I live), we can improve our national image overseas and at the same time make an enlarged foreign aid program less burdensome. Similarly, we ought to speed up the pace of desegregation of our schools and housing, because it is the right thing to do, and because millions of Latin Americans (and Africans and Asians) with dark skins are watching us. The Negro historian W. E. B. DuBois warned us, as far back as 1903, that "the problem of the Twentieth Century is the problem of the color line," and our accomplishments in breaking down that barrier are not keeping pace with our international responsibilities. Every audience I lectured to in Lima, Buenos Aires, and Rio de Janeiro was anxious to question me about Governor Faubus and Little Rock, and Fidel Castro's *Prensa Latina* news agency sees to it that even illiterate Latin

Americans with radios heard about the uproar into which one
Negro college student threw the sovereign state of Mississippi.
The United States Information Service, partially recovered from
the crippling blows of the McCarthy era, is doing a better job
under Edward R. Murrow than before. But even the ablest public
relations men in the world cannot succeed in the long run unless
they have a good product to push. Latin Americans, surveying
the wreck of Kennedy's legislative programs, may well wonder
if it isn't the United States which needs to be freed from an
oligarchy.

17. Finally, it is important for us to face up to the realities
of Latin American geographic, economic, social, and political
problems, and to understand that we cannot solve them with the
ballyhoo tactics of American advertising or the skillful ghost
writers of the New Frontier. It may be that President Kennedy
really understood that the high hopes he raised in his initial
speeches on the *Alianza* were doomed to disappointment, that
he was only trying to create a mood in which something, at least,
could be accomplished. If so, disillusionment was not long in
coming. After Moscoso's memorandum about difficulties "staggering and frustrating beyond endurance" came a Congressional
attempt to slash the program which Frank M. Coffin, Deputy
Chief of AID, termed "a colossal breach of faith," and the subsequent resignation of AID chief Fowler Hamilton. All in all, as
the first annual report of the Committee of Nine appointed to
appraise the program confessed, Latin economies were still in
a state of "quasi-stagnation" and the program had "not yet had
the political and psychological impact it should have provoked."
Some of these disappointments could have been avoided if
we had not set our hopes so high in the first place; it might have
been better to have aimed at an easier target, and to have been
sure of hitting it. Our political position requires us to take some
responsibility for the progress of *all* the underdeveloped countries of the world; we are not going to abandon our aid programs
in India, in the emerging African nations, in such especially
strategic countries as South Korea, South Viet Nam, and Formosa.

This involves us with some (rather vague) sort of responsibility to help improve the well-being of more than one billion people (soon to be one and one-half or two billion), most of them illiterate and unskilled, and most of them living in areas without the agricultural potential and mineral wealth of the United States and Western Europe. Even if we adopt all the foregoing suggestions on a world-wide scale, massive poverty is going to be with us for a long time to come. We are not impotent, of course, but we are not omnipotent either; it is clear that many underdeveloped countries will be "beggar nations" for the rest of our lifetimes no matter what anybody does to help them.

These seventeen suggestions are not, of course, meant to have the binding force of the Ten Commandments or the Fourteen Points. Some of them are far more important than others; others might easily be added. The point is that there is no single, sure, infallible cure for Latin America's manifold ills, and that even if there were, nobody is in a position to put it into effect. Advocates of unlimited free enterprise such as Barry Goldwater and partisans of violent social revolution such as Fidel Castro are both too unsophisticated about economic affairs and too sanguine about our ability to shape events to suit ourselves. President Kennedy, at least, after the disappointments of his first year in office, seems to be willing to accept the limitations of his power, to make fewer grandiose promises, to operate at a less intense and dedicated pace (though no president has ever worked harder). Perhaps during the remainder of his years in office he will be able to translate his unmatchable skill in domestic politics into an equally shrewd and pragmatic policy for Latin America.

Students of Latin American affairs will recognize that my list of suggestions contains little that is new; it is largely familiar material, stale stuff that people with more experience than I have been saying for years. The only reason for repeating these truisms is that they are, after all, true and important and that many of them have been ignored for years by the men who have made our foreign policy. Even when recognized by Kennedy and his advisers, they may not be put into practice because vested interests, inertia, Congressional opposition, and public ignorance and indifference stand in the way. The Soviet *bloc,* checked in Western Europe by the Common Market and torn asunder in Asia by the quarrel between Mao and Khrushchev, may see in the Cuban experience an opportunity to carry out its apocalyptic schemes of a Communist revolution in every country between Cape Horn and the Rio Grande. And Latin America, with its vast resources in oil, iron ore, copper, and the products of tropical agriculture, and with its rapidly expanding population made up of people who demand a better way of life, is clearly a decisive area and clearly in danger. Should *fidelismo* prove to be the way of the future in the nations to the south of us, the Cold War will be over, and we shall have lost it.

Index